ENGLISH
FOR KEY
STAGE 3

LANGUAGE
INCORPORATED
1

ENGLISH
FOR KEY
STAGE 3

LANGUAGE INCORPORATED

LANGUAGE
INCORPORATED
1

NIGEL KENT
MICK BURTON

STANLEY THORNES (PUBLISHERS) LTD

First published in 1991 by:
Stanley Thornes (Publishers) Ltd
Old Station Drive
Leckhampton
CHELTENHAM GL53 0DN
England

British Library Cataloguing in Publication Data
Kent, Nigel
    Language incorporated: Book 1: English for key
    stage 3.
    I. Title   II. Burton, Mick
    428

    ISBN 0-7487-0573-2

Typeset by Tech-Set, Gateshead, Tyne and Wear
Printed and bound in Hong Kong

Contents

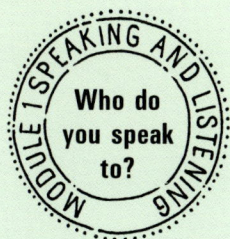

Introduction

To the student

Welcome to *Language Incorporated*! We hope you will enjoy the English work in this book, which will take you through Year 7.

Do read the contents list! You will find a range of modules in Speaking and Listening, Reading and Writing. In each module you will not only practise your language skills, but you will also be asked to think about the language you use and meet in everyday life. You will be amazed at how much you already know about language. By following this course you will add to that knowledge and, in doing so, we hope you will become more confident and more skilful in your own use of language.

To the teacher

Language Incorporated is a fully integrated course for Key Stage Three English. Its aim is to provide material which will facilitate:

1 Speaking and Listening

'The development of pupils' understanding of the spoken word and the capacity to express themselves effectively in a variety of speaking and listening activities, matching style and response to audience and purpose.'

Cox 15, 18

2 Reading

'The development of the ability to read, understand and respond to all types of writing; the development of reading and information-retrieval strategies for the purposes of study; the development of knowledge about language.'

Cox 16, 1

3 Writing

'A growing ability to construct and convey meaning in written language matching to audience and purpose.'

Cox 17, 23

Each module focuses on one Profile Component as a base, with activities from other Profile Components built in. This will make a balanced programme of English which delivers National Curriculum targets in accordance with the Programmes of Study requirements. Each unit in the modules contains material which covers the attainment targets specified in the grids printed alongside the contents list. A range of statements of attainment is suggested for each unit. In practice it will depend on the class composition and ability range which levels are taught. Presentation, AT 4/5, is regarded as a necessary permeation issue. In the pupil's book it is dealt with as a component part of the writing process and highlighted in reference to drafting.

The teacher's guide that accompanies this book contains a detailed account of the model of language which underscores *Language Incorporated*. It shows how to relate concepts and activities in a perspective of pupils' development as users of language, by:

1 pointing out the aspects of language which each module/unit covers

2 providing consolidation/extension activities for each module

3 covering in more detail aspects of presentation.

Key to symbols used for pupils' work:

= Individual work

= Pair work

= Group work

= Class work

1 Finding the right words

The speaking and listening survey

Who do you speak to? When? Why?
Who do you listen to? When? Why?

These questions are the focus of this module. To help you think about some of the answers you need to do some research, on your own to begin with. Think back over the last 48 hours. Note down every time you were speaking or listening – every time!

Here is an example to start you off.

Introduction

Speaking and listening are language activities which come naturally. As a very young child you listened to all the sounds around you. You then began to speak and you probably have not stopped since.

In this module you will be thinking about speaking and listening as ways of learning, at home and at school. You will be developing your speaking and listening skills through different activities; sometimes you will be working with a partner, sometimes in a group.

48 HOURS SPEAKING AND LISTENING

SPEAKING	PLACE OF SPEAKING	REASONS FOR SPEAKING	TIME SPENT SPEAKING
Questions	Home	Need breakfast	10 secs
Orders	Home/garden	Stop dog barking	20 secs
Telling a story	On the way to school	Need to tell your mates about your narrow escape	2 mins
Expressing feelings	Playground	Friend given detention	4 mins
Responding to questions	Classroom	Teacher asks class questions about homework	15 secs

Use the same headings for listening.
When you have completed your survey get into small groups.
Number them 1–6.

THINK ABOUT THE TIMES AND PLACES WHEN YOU SPEAK OR LISTEN. WHAT DO YOU LEARN BY SPEAKING AND LISTENING?

Discuss

Groups 1–5: Talk about the results of your survey. Group 6 should send one member to groups 1–5. He or she should act as a messenger and reporter. After 15 minutes, Group 6 members should present their report from the group they have been with to the rest of the class.

Guidelines for messengers/reporters

▶ Listen carefully to the group you are reporting on.

▶ Write down the most important ideas they come up with.
▶ Read back your report to the group.
▶ Make sure they agree it is a fair report of their ideas.
▶ Report in a clear voice to the rest of the class.

All groups might find these questions helpful when sorting out what to do and say:

▶ What type of speaking do you do most?
▶ How often do you listen without speaking?
▶ Which type of speaking do you most/least enjoy?
▶ What sorts of reasons do you have for speaking/listening?
▶ When do you do most of your speaking/listening?
▶ Where do you do most of your speaking/listening?
▶ What do you think is the most/least important speaking/listening activity you do?
▶ What is the most interesting/surprising thing you have learned about your speaking/listening habits from doing this survey?

Project; record and reflect

All your lessons at school involve language. Sometimes you listen, sometimes you speak. In each case you are helping yourself to learn your subjects by listening and speaking carefully and **appropriately**. The way in which you would discuss whether Mr Gorbachev was right to allow freedom to Russian TV would be different from the way in which you would discuss the latest soap opera!

To help you reflect on speaking and listening, and how you can develop these skills, you can make and keep a speaking/listening log. You need:

▶ an exercise book
▶ your favourite pen or pencil
▶ regular time, in school and at home, to write down your thoughts.

Think about these questions:

▶ Do I ever answer the teacher's questions?
▶ Do I ever volunteer information in lessons?
▶ Do I ask questions if I do not understand the subject?
▶ In group or pair work, how do I get on with other people? Can I express my ideas clearly? Can I persuade other people that my ideas are good?

2 Words slip, slide . . .

You now need to think about the **words** you choose when you speak.

FIRST DAY AT SCHOOL

A millionbillionwillion miles from home
Waiting for the bell to go. (To go where?)
Why are they all so big, other children?
So noisy? So much at home they
must have been born in uniform.
Lived all their lives in playgrounds.
Spent the years inventing games
that don't let me in. Games
that are rough, that swallow you up.

And the railings.
All around, the railings.
Are they to keep out wolves and monsters?
Things that carry off and eat children?
Things you don't take sweets from?
Perhaps they're to stop us getting out.
Running away from the lessins. Lessin.
What does a lessin look like?
Sounds small and slimy.
They keep them in glassrooms.
Whole rooms made out of glass. Imagine.

I wish I could remember my name.
Mummy said it would come in useful.
Like wellies. When there's puddles.
Yellowwellies. I wish she was here.
I think my name is sewn on somewhere.
Perhaps the teachers will read it for me.
Tea-cher. The one who makes the tea.

Roger McGough

They picked me up bodily, kicking and bawling, and carried me up to the road.

'Boys who don't go to school get put into boxes, and turn into rabbits, and get chopped up Sundays.'

I felt this was overdoing it rather, but I said no more after that. I arrived at the school just three feet tall and fatly wrapped in my scarves. The playground roared like a rodeo, and the potato burned through my thigh. Old boots, ragged stockings, torn trousers and skirts, went skating and skidding around me. The rabble closed in; I was encircled; grit flew in my face like shrapnel. Tall girls with frizzled hair, and huge boys with sharp elbows, began to prod me with hideous interest. They plucked at my scarves, spun me round like a top, screwed my nose, and stole my potato.

I was rescued at last by a gracious lady – the sixteen-year-old junior-teacher – who boxed a few ears and dried my face and led me off to The Infants. I spent that first day picking holes in paper, then went home in a smouldering temper.

'What's the matter, Loll? Didn't he like it at school, then?'

'They never gave me the present!'

'Present? What present?'

'They said they'd give me a present.'

'Well, now, I'm sure they didn't.'

'They did! They said: "You're Laurie Lee, ain't you? Well, just you sit there for the present." I sat there all day but I never got it. I ain't going back there again!'

From *Cider with Rosie*, Laurie Lee

When you speak, do other people listen?
Do you have problems with words, like Laurie Lee?
Remember to note down in your logs when there is something you need to get right, or when you have succeeded in solving a problem with speaking and listening.

YOU NEED TO MAKE WORDS YOUR OWN. BUT YOU ALSO NEED TO UNDERSTAND HOW MEANING CHANGES ACROSS TIME AND SUBJECT.

MODULE 1 SPEAKING AND LISTENING

LANGUAGE NOTE

Words are very lively; they do not just lie still in a dictionary and mean the same for ever.

Alice and the Mad Hatter are having a problem in agreeing on the meaning of the word 'time'. Read the extract from *Alice's Adventures in Wonderland* and, with a partner, work out how you could help them to understand each other.

Alice had been looking over his shoulder with some curiosity. 'What a funny watch!' she remarked. 'It tells the day of the month, and doesn't tell what o'clock it is!'

'Why should it?' muttered the Hatter. 'Does *your* watch tell you what year it is?'

'Of course not,' Alice replied very readily, 'but that's because it stays the same year for such a long time together.'

'Which is just the case with *mine*,' said the Hatter.

Alice felt dreadfully puzzled. The Hatter's remark seemed to have no sort of meaning in it, and yet it was certainly English. 'I don't quite understand you,' she said, as politely as she could.

'The Dormouse is asleep again,' said the Hatter, and he poured a little hot tea upon its nose.

The Dormouse shook its head impatiently, and said, without opening its eyes, 'Of course, of course; just what I was going to remark myself.'

'Have you guessed the riddle yet?' the Hatter said, turning to Alice again.

'No, I give it up,' Alice replied. 'What's the answer?'

'I haven't the slightest idea,' said the Hatter.

'Nor I,' said the March Hare.

Alice sighed wearily. 'I think you might do something better with the time,' she said, 'than waste it in asking riddles that have no answers.'

'If you knew Time as well as I do,' said the Hatter, 'you wouldn't talk about wasting *it*. It's *him*.'

'I don't know what you mean,' said Alice.

'Of course you don't!' the Hatter said, tossing his head contemptuously. 'I dare say you never even spoke to Time!'

'Perhaps not,' Alice cautiously replied, 'but I know I have to beat time when I learn music.'

'Ah! that accounts for it,' said the Hatter. 'He won't stand beating. Now, if you only kept on good terms with him, he'd do almost anything you liked with the clock. For instance, suppose it were nine o'clock in the morning, just time to begin lessons: you'd only have to whisper a hint to Time, and round goes the clock in a twinkling! Half-past one, time for dinner!'

('I only wish it was,' the March Hare said to itself in a whisper.)

'That would be grand, certainly,' said Alice thoughtfully. 'But then – I shouldn't be hungry for it, you know.'

'Not at first, perhaps,' said the Hatter, 'but you could keep it to half-past one as long as you liked.'

'Is that the way *you* manage?' Alice asked.

From *Alice's Adventures in Wonderland*, Lewis Carroll

Look back at language

When you are in the library, look for the words 'nice' and 'naughty' in a large dictionary. Find out how their meanings have changed since they were first used.

Have any of you been to a hospital? This word originally meant a place of entertainment; then it became used for the places used by military monks, the Knights Hospitallers, who used to provide shelter and care for the pilgrims to the Holy Land. From them came the meaning of hospital we have today.

English is a language which has developed over many centuries. Lots of words have come into England as a result of invasions. The main ones are from:

▶ the Angles, Saxons and Jutes (ask your history teacher about these)
▶ St Augustine, who converted this country to Christianity (this was not an invasion, of course)
▶ William the Conqueror, who forced Norman French upon English speakers.

As part of your ongoing log entries, try to find a word a week which comes from a language other than English. You will hear and read lots of words in your other subjects which come from Greek or Latin. To start with find out what the names of these subjects mean, and which languages they come from:

▶ History   ▶ Science
▶ Geography   ▶ English.
▶ Mathematics

Try to find out what the names of **all** your school subjects mean. Here are some examples of borrowed words which you might know:

▶ sheep, shepherd, ox, earth, plough are all from the Anglo-Saxons. What other farming words do you know which you can look up in a large
▶ dictionary?
disciple, monk, pope, angel, devil, all come from Christianity, which used words from languages like Latin, Greek, Hebrew and even Sanskrit.
▶ felony, perjury, attorney, bailiff and nobility all come from Norman French. If you do not know some of these words, look them up in a large dictionary.

Discuss and write

Language is changing all around you. In groups, discuss which words you use between yourselves, but not to your parents or teachers. Select ten of these to put in a time capsule for 2091, and write their meanings down. Remember that readers in the future will need crystal clear explanations.

There is a follow up exercise to this one in Module 2: Reading.

How difficult was that task? Does writing meanings down involve a different sort of language activity from sharing them with someone you are speaking to? Think about this and make some short notes in your log about the differences between speaking, listening and writing as you go through the next half term. Think about:
▶ the need for someone to listen when you speak
▶ the way in which someone you are speaking to can switch off and show you if it is boring – what happens then?
▶ the need you have as a writer to make details clear to your reader
▶ the need to know who is going to read your writing
▶ the need to choose your words very carefully when you write, because your audience is not present with you.

Research, record and reflect

In your other school subjects you will meet lots of new words. Some of them are quite easy to understand, like Brontosaurus.

Some of them may be words you recognise, but their meanings are different from what you expect. Look at 'set' for example:
▶ game, **set** and match
▶ you are in **set** two for maths
▶ the jam had a poor **set**
▶ the badger was cleaning out his **set**.

Make a small dictionary for each of your school subjects. Put in:

1 New words
2 Common words used in special ways in each subject.

Compare your dictionary with a partner's at the end of each term.

Plundering words

Since English has taken words from many other languages, it is useful for you to know about how some words, which come from Latin and Greek, are built up. Why? Because you will meet many of them in other subjects, such as science, geography, history, or mathematics.

Some you can recognise because they have **prefixes** at the beginning of the word. And what is a prefix? Look at the words precede, predict, prehistoric, prelude, premonition. What is common to all of them? The prefix *pre* – it comes from Latin and means 'before', or 'in front'.

Look at these words now: postscript, postnatal, postmortem, postpone. Common to all of these is the prefix *post* – it is Latin for 'after', or 'following on'.

Check the meaning of all these words in a large dictionary. When you are in other subject lessons, make a note of the words which are built up using prefixes. Add the ones you are most interested in to your language log.

There will be more on word building in Module 4: Speaking and Listening.

③ This story of yours

When you tell someone about something you have done, something you have seen, or something that has happened to you, you are telling a story.

Read aloud and discuss

when I was . . . when I was . . . I lived down old end and I was only about four or five and erm I was on this little motorbike thing and er . . . yer know one o' these small uns and I had a big pencil in mi mouth yer know one o' the big thick ones and erm I fell off the mo . . . I fell off it and it was in mi mouth and the . . . and it . . . it it hit the floor and it went straight into mi gum up the top and the . . . and it nearly went down mi mouth and I could have choked but it . . . it just hit the gum . . . any way I went to hospital and I . . . when I come back out I had a big hole in mi gum.

Take it in turns to read Ian's story aloud. While one person is reading, the rest should think about these questions:

▶ How does Ian set the scene?
▶ What is the action?
▶ What is the result?
▶ How does Ian make a viewpoint on his story?

Look at his choice of words and his comments on his accident.

Now each person tell the rest of the group a story about themselves. It does not have to be fantastic, or brilliant, or heroic. But make it honest. It could be about your pet cat (dog, parrot, python, etc.),

THINK ABOUT YOUR VOICE AND WHAT YOU DO WITH IT. HOW DO YOU TELL A STORY? WHATS THE DIFFERENCE BETWEEN TELLING AND WRITING?

your brother/sister, mum/dad, uncle/aunt, or anybody. It could be about something that happened to you, or to someone else. It could be about something you saw or heard. Try to make a viewpoint on your story by choosing your words very carefully.

The next step is to decide on the story everybody likes best in your groups. Then write it down, choosing the clearest writer, **just as it was told. Use the exact words of the teller.** When you write down the story, you should discuss some of the problems of writing down spoken language.

Guidelines for writing down speech

► Do not worry about spelling in this case – if someone says 'beuk' for 'book', write it down as 'beuk'.

► If someone stops to say 'er' or 'um' put it in.

► If someone says 'could of' instead of 'could have' put it in.

► Make sure you show the emphasis on the words that people say by underlining. Try saying to a partner 'I can't make bread' as many different ways as you can and see if, between you, you can work out

the different meanings for each version. This is called **intonation**, and it is a very important part of the way we organise our spoken language. You can think about intonation in some of the work you do later in all the modules.

Look at the poem 'bacun rind' by Barry Heath to see an example of spoken language written down.

bacun rind

ah w'stood waitin
foh medad t'finish
iz breakfust
soas ah cudd ayiz
bacun rind
an
ah Lez stood beindme
an
medad sez
'Gerraht!
yowad yorn yesterdi.'
an
ah joined
tomorras
que.

Barry Heath

What differences between spoken and written language have you noticed in your work so far?

Keep a note of the most important differences in your log; do not forget to look at other school subjects as well as English.

4 'He do the Police in different voices'

Impersonation is one of the few things which Sloppy, a character in Charles Dickens' novel *Our Mutual Friend*, can do well. What about you? Who or what can you impersonate?

Discuss

Which voices do you like best? Think about radio, TV, school, home. When you listen to people speaking, whose voices do you like most/least, and why? Discuss this in your groups and make a list with these headings:

NAME	LIKE	DISLIKE	NEUTRAL	REASON

One group should act as messengers/reporters, and present the findings of the other groups to the class.

LANGUAGE NOTE

One reason you may like or dislike a person's voice is because of their *accent*. It is difficult to prevent this. There are no real reasons for saying one accent is better than another. The problem is that we learn language in our families and communities where the accent is often the same across a large area. So we get used to some accents, and we think of others as foreign, or posh, or inferior.

Accent is the way we pronounce words. Try saying bath, grass, us, father, nasty, book, away, you . . .

Everyone has an accent; it is part of their voiceprint, like a fingerprint. Which accent you have depends on where you live. It does not make any difference to your ability to use language. (See the Language Note on p. 15.)

Hear my cry!

What do you do with your voice? When you speak do other people understand you?

Discuss and write

Your voice is a very important part of *you*. It is the only one you have got, but it can be really versatile. In pairs, make a list of the things you can do with your voice.

What did you have in your list? Some of the following? Talk, shout, whisper, shriek, cry, snap, mumble, grumble, hiss, roar.

Try speaking the words 'I want my breakfast' in some of the ways we have listed above. Check with your teacher first about disturbing other classes!

Write

You can make poems from a list like the one above. Take some or all of these words, and others of your own, and write a poem about using your voice. Here are two lines as an example:

I whisper when the darkness falls, 'Who's there?'
I shout if Liverpool win again.

What do you need to know to write your voice poems?

► First, put down all your ideas as quickly as you can.
► Look again and if some ideas do not seem right cross them off.
► Think about the details of your list of voice activities – when do you shout? Do you shout at the top of your voice?
► Think about the lines; they should have a beat, or rhythm, to them. Try saying these groups of words in different ways till you hear their rhythm:

I wandered quietly by the sea
She sang her songs as sweet as a nightingale
O what a lovely war
To be, or not to be
Do not go gentle into that good night
Ash on an old man's sleeve

► Try to make each line contain a picture for the reader to think about.
► Build the lines into the order you think sounds right for your poem.

Discuss

Ask a partner to read your first version. Ask him or her for suggestions to make it sound better.
When you look at each other's writing you should check on:

► choice of words – are they the best for the job?
► how the words fit together – do they make sense?
► the lines – do they have a beat? Are they too short or too long?
► the poem as a whole piece of writing – does it stick together well?

Looking at these points should help you to improve the first version. When you have completed the poems, read them around the group. Each person should find at least one point to praise and one point to criticise. Listening to each other's work is an important part of your own learning about language. You can help each other to improve your skills.

CAN YOU IMPERSONATE OTHER VOICES? WHAT IS YOUR ACCE

Read and perform

In groups read the extract from *Woof*. Decide who is going to read which part. Read the extract aloud. Try to vary your voice as you read until you have the best sound for the reading. Swap parts so that everyone has a chance to be Eric the dog.

At that moment Alison Jukes came riding up on her bicycle, followed closely by Joan Spooner on hers. They were friends again, it seemed.

'Hello, Malky!' said Alison.

'It's that dog again!' said Joan.

'And he wants y'rock,' Alison said.

Whereupon Malky immediately snatched it away and took a bit himself. Eric, with mixed feelings, trotted over to join Kenny and Roy. Having failed to agree a swop, they were kicking the ball back and forth between them.

Joan said, 'Whose dog is he really?'

'He's not telling,' said Kenny. 'I don't think he knows.'

'I know,' said Roy. 'I know more than you think.' He turned his attention to Malky. 'I'll give you half this apple for a bite of rock.'

Malky studied the apple.

'Don't you, Malky,' said Alison. 'You keep it.'

'Ask him whose dog it is,' said Kenny.

Then Roy had an idea. 'Listen, Malky – if you give me a bite, this dog'll shake hands with you.' He crouched and whispered to Eric, 'Go on, Eric, be a sport!'

Eric considered the matter. He could see that Roy was getting carried away; also, by rights, if any rock *was* going, *he* should get it. Then again . . . He looked across at Malky's little beaming face, and he thought, 'Why not?'

Eric approached Malky, who by this time had left his tricycle and joined the others on the grass.

'On the command "shake hands",' said Roy, 'this dog will . . . shake hands.' Then he said, 'Shake . . . hands!'

Eric at once held out his paw. For a moment Malky was overcome with shyness, but of course he was delighted, too. Soon he was holding Eric's paw in his own sticky hand and shaking it proudly.

'There!' said Roy. 'Now, on the command "bite rock", this boy will . . .' Roy got his rock, though the amount was carefully monitored by Kenny. After that there was a general rush to see what else Eric could do.

'Get him to say "How do you do?",' said Joan.

'Like that Australian dog,' Kenny said.

'Get him to count!' said Alison.

Roy – flushed with success – got Eric to count. 'What's two plus two?' he said.

'Woof, woof, woof, woof!' barked Eric. (*He* was getting carried away.)

'Six take away four?' said Roy.

'Woof, woof!'

'The square root of nine?' (Roy was good at maths.)

'Woof, woof, woof!' (So was Eric.)

It was about now that Kenny and Alison exchanged puzzled looks. They realized something was going on (so did Joan), but couldn't quite tell what it was.

'It's a trick,' said Alison.

'No it's not; he's just a brainy dog,' said Roy.

Then Joan said, 'All right then – what's four hundred and ninety-six plus two hundred and eighty-three?'

Eric hardly hesitated. 'Woof, woof, woof, woof, woof, woof, woof –'

'Hang on, hang on,' said Roy. 'We'll be here for ever.'

'What's the capital of Peru?' said Kenny.

'What's the time?' said Joan.

Eric made no reply but continued to look expectantly at his audience. It was as though he was waiting for a question he *could* answer, which, in truth, he was. He hadn't had this much attention since his tenth birthday.

Roy said, 'Wait a minute; let me have a go.' And he said, 'Here's a good 'un: Which of these girls do y'like the best – her or her?'

Eric cocked his head on one side, then the other. He looked Joan and Alison up and down. The first thought in his mind was, 'Neither!' However, secretly (so secretly he hadn't even told Roy, though Roy knew anyway) Alison was his favourite. (And of course, *she* knew as well.)

While Eric was seeming to make his mind up, Kenny said, 'How's he going to choose?'

'He can point,' said Joan.

'That's it,' Roy said; 'point!'

And so, eventually, Eric put out his paw and pointed at Alison. She laughed. 'He *is* a brainy dog!' she said. And then, 'Have a crisp!'

After this the gathering began to break up. Kenny had to take Malky home and get ready for the sports. Joan and Alison needed to collect their kit.

As she rode off, Alison tossed a final crisp to Eric. He, despite its wayward flight through the air, caught it and crunched it up.

As she rode off, Joan called out, 'Whose dog is he *really*? What's his name?'

Roy paused for a second and said, 'Eric.'

'What?'

'Eric.'

'I can't hear you!'

'It's just as well,' said Roy. He watched Joan disappear through the gates. 'You'd never believe it.'

From *Woof*, A. Ahlberg

YOU CAN MAKE A POEM FROM IDEAS ON YOUR VOICE.

5 Don't interrupt!

Sometimes it is difficult to speak at all because the other person is doing all the talking. Read the poem below. It was written by someone at school.

Don't
Don't
Don't
Don't

Don't Interrupt!

Turn the television down!
None of your cheek!
Sit down!
Shut up!
Don't make a fool of yourself!
Respect your elders!
I can't put up with you anymore!
Go outside.
Don't walk so fast!
Don't run.
Don't forget to brush your teeth!
Don't forget to polish your shoes!
Don't slam the door!
Have manners!
Don't interrupt when I'm talking!
Put your hand over your mouth when you cough.
Don't talk with your mouth full!
Go to the market with me.
You spend too much money!
No more pocket money for you dear.
Go to your room!
Don't stuff yourself with sweets!
Don't point!
Don't go too near the television.
You are not coming out until you have tidied your room.
Don't interrupt when I'm talking!
Did you get any homework today?
Always carry a pen to school.
Eat your dinner up.
Wear your school uniform!
Turn the television over to watch 'Dallas'.
Bring any letters home from school.
Come straight home tomorrow.
Tidy your bed.
Don't shout!
Don't listen to my conversation.
Don't look at the sun it could blind you.
Don't bite your nails!
Don't suck your thumb!
Why don't you answer me!
You never listen to a word I say!
Don't interrupt when I'm talking!

Demetroulla Vassili

Sit down!
shut up!
Don't run
Don't point
Don't shout

THINK ABOUT GETTING A WORD IN WHEN SOMEONE TALKS TOO MUCH. EXPLORE SOME SCENES WHEN YOU CAN'T SAY WHAT YOU WANT.

6 But what I really think is . . .

Point of view

You have looked at speaking in different situations. Each time someone speaks to someone else, they have a point of view, a way of seeing that situation. Remember Ian's story; he made his point of view clear by choosing his words carefully.

Look back at your speaking/listening survey; the audience is important when you are speaking. Who you speak to changes the sorts of words you choose and the ways in which you arrange them in groups or sentences.

Read and discuss

Read the passages from Maya Angelou's story about her childhood. With a partner identify the differences between Momma's words to the dentist in each passage and then work out how her point of view changes from passage A to passage B. Do the same for the dentist's words.

Does passage B really happen? If you think it does not, why?

A

Momma knocked on the back door and a young white girl opened it to show surprise at seeing us there. Momma said she wanted to see Dentist Lincoln and to tell him Annie was there. The girl closed the door firmly. Now the humiliation of hearing Momma describe herself as if she had no last name to the young white girl was equal to the physical pain. It seemed terribly unfair to have a toothache and a headache and have to bear at the same time the heavy burden of Blackness.

It was always possible that the teeth would quiet down and maybe drop out of their own accord. Momma said we would wait. We leaned in the harsh sunlight on the shaky railings of the dentist's back porch for over an hour.

He opened the door and looked at Momma. 'Well, Annie, what can I do for you?'

He didn't see the towel around my jaw or notice my swollen face.

Momma said, 'Dentist Lincoln. It's my grandbaby here. She got two rotten teeth that's giving her a fit.' She waited for him to acknowledge the truth of her statement. He made no comment, orally or facially.

'She had this toothache purt' near four days now, and today I said, "Young lady, you going to the Dentist."'

'Annie?'

'Yes, sir, Dentist Lincoln.'

He was choosing words the way people hunt for shells. 'Annie, you know I don't treat nigra, colored people.'

'I know, Dentist Lincoln. But this here is just my little grandbaby, and she ain't gone be no trouble to you . . .'

'Annie, everybody has a policy. In this world you have to have a policy. Now, my policy is I don't treat colored people.'

The sun had baked the oil out of Momma's skin and melted the Vaseline in her hair. She shone greasily as she leaned out of the dentist's shadow.

'Seem like to me, Dentist Lincoln, you might look after her, she ain't nothing but a little mite. And seems like maybe you owe me a favor or two.'

He reddened slightly. 'Favor or no favor. The money has all been repaid to you and that's the end of it. Sorry, Annie.' He had his hand on the doorknob. 'Sorry.' His voice was a bit kinder on the second 'Sorry,' as if he really was.

Momma said, 'I wouldn't press on you like this for myself but I can't take No. Not for my grandbaby. When you come to borrow my money you didn't have to beg. You asked me, and I lent it. Now, it wasn't my policy. I ain't no moneylender, but you stood to lose this building and I tried to help you out.'

'It's been paid, and raising your voice won't make me change my mind. My policy . . .' He let go of the door and stepped nearer Momma. The three of us were crowded on the small landing. 'Annie, my policy is I'd rather stick my hand in a dog's mouth than in a nigger's.'

He had never once looked at me. He turned his back and went through the door into the cool beyond. Momma backed up inside herself for a few minutes. I forgot everything except her face which was almost a new one to me. She leaned over and took the doorknob, and in her everyday soft voice she said, 'Sister, go on downstairs. Wait for me. I'll be there directly.'

B

Momma walked in that room as if she owned it. She shoved that silly nurse aside with one hand and strode into the dentist's office. He was sitting in his chair, sharpening his mean instruments and putting extra sting into his medicines. Her eyes were blazing like live coals and her arms had doubled themselves in length. He looked up at her just before she caught him by the collar of his white jacket.

'Stand up when you see a lady, you contemptuous scoundrel.' Her tongue had thinned and the words rolled off well enunciated. Enunciated and sharp like little claps of thunder.

The dentist had no choice but to stand at R.O.T.C. attention. His head dropped after a minute and his voice was humble. 'Yes, ma'am, Mrs. Henderson.'

'You knave, do you think you acted like a gentleman, speaking to me like that in front of my granddaughter?' She didn't shake him, although she had the power. She simply held him upright.

'No, ma'am, Mrs. Henderson.'

'No, ma'am, Mrs. Henderson, what?' Then she did give him the tiniest of shakes, but because of her strength the action set his head and arms to shaking loose on the ends of his body. He stuttered much worse than Uncle Willie. 'No, ma'am, Mrs. Henderson, I'm sorry.'

With just an edge of her disgust showing, Momma slung him back in his dentist's chair. 'Sorry is as sorry does, and you're about the sorriest dentist I ever laid my eyes on.'

From *I Know Why the Caged Bird Sings*, Maya Angelou

Maya Angelou is a black writer who lives in the USA. She experienced the language both of her community and of the white Americans. Both communities had very strong viewpoints on life and its problems. Maya's grandmother found that the dentist was fixed in his viewpoint. You will be looking at the language of such prejudice in later modules.

Discuss

What do you feel strongly about? Identify five issues which you think are very important to life in the next hundred years.

Some of these might seem important to you:

▶ the greenhouse effect
▶ overpopulation
▶ hunger and poverty
▶ space exploration
▶ happiness
▶ transport
▶ crime
▶ racial prejudice
▶ equality between women and men
▶ education.

Discuss the ways in which language helps or hinders the expression of your ideas and feelings about these issues. Is it possible to talk about them without having a point of view?

Presentation

Using your messenger/reporter system with the groups, produce posters which will be part of the class campaign to make the rest of the school aware of the things that are important for life in the twenty-first century.

In your posters you should aim to:

▶ Identify your issue, for example, Saving the Whale.
▶ State your viewpoint clearly.
▶ Illustrate your viewpoint with photographs or drawings which make your language have a greater impact on the reader of the poster.

LOOK CAREFULLY AT HOW YOU CAN EXPRESS A POINT OF VIEW. WHAT DO YOU FEEL STRONGLY ABOUT?

7 The TV kids

Viewing and scripting

Discuss

Watch an episode from a favourite soap opera. Discuss how the action is scripted so that we see it from different characters' points of view. You could look at one incident or event and see how the viewpoint of the characters is created by the script. Concentrate on the words the characters use.

Discuss and write

In groups, make up an incident or event for an episode of a soap opera or TV serial. Then write the script, showing the different points of view which each character, or group of characters has, on the incident. Choose your words carefully!

To help you along, here is a sample plot planner.

	SCENE 1	SCENE 2
PLACE	IN BAR OF QUEEN VIC	IN ALBERT SQUARE
TIME	LUNCHTIME	EARLY AFTERNOON
CHARACTERS	PETE, CLYDE, PAT A STRANGER	DOT, TWO POLICE OFFICERS
ACTION	PETE IS TALKING ABOUT A QUIZ AGAINST THE ROSE AND CROWN. HE IS CONFIDENT OF WINNING. PAT IS NOT LISTENING. PETE NOTICES A STRANGER LISTENING TO HIM. STRANGER LEAVES IN A HURRY. CLYDE SAYS THE STRANGER IS FROM THE ROSE AND CROWN. PETE LOOKS WORRIED	POLICE ENTER DOT'S HOUSE. DOT IS NERVOUS AND WILL NOT ANSWER THEIR QUESTIONS ABOUT THE MISSING BABY. POLICE OFFICER NOTICES BABY'S CARDIGAN BEHING CHAIR. DOT GRABS IT, SOBBING. OUTSIDE, POLICE DISCUSS THEIR SUSPICIONS.

LOOK AT HOW YOUR FAVOURITE TV SOAP OPERAS WORK. TRY YOUR OWN SCRIPT.

8 Bang!

Now you have to use your imagination and some clear thinking. You are on a car ferry going to France. A terrorist group telegraphs the captain that a bomb has been placed on board. It is in a small cupboard on the car deck which is too small for adults to enter. A bomb disposal expert is in contact with the ship by telephone. Your best friend volunteers to enter the cupboard and defuse the bomb following instructions which **you** have to give him/her, because the telephone only reaches the cupboard door.

Read and discuss

Here is a diagram of the bomb. You have to instruct your friend to defuse it.

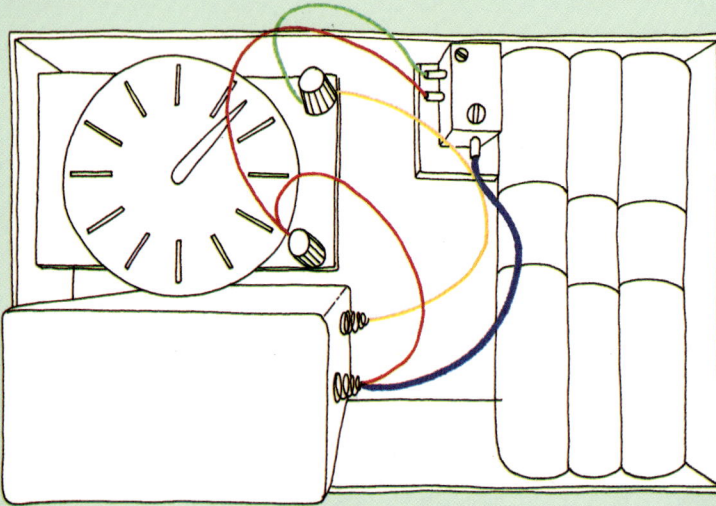

INFORMATION FOR DEFUSING THE BOMB

Follow these steps in the order stated: any deviation will blow the bomb up.

1 Describe the box and the location of the parts of the bomb.
2 Pull green wire out from TIMER slowly; don't shake the timer.
3 Cut yellow wire at timer end.
4 Loosen the thin red wire from the battery terminal.
5 Cut the thick blue wire very quickly.

Discuss and write

Work with a partner who should have pencil and paper. Spend two minutes memorising these instructions and then shut the book. Tell your partner the instructions slowly and clearly so he or she can write them down. Then swop: your partner should memorise the instructions, tell them to you; you write them down. Compare your notes. Who was safe? Who got blown up?

Sometimes it is vital to be absolutely accurate in your speaking and listening.

Discuss

With a partner discuss what other situations call for really accurate uses of language.

What difference does it make if you write down the necessary words? Does it help, or can there be problems? Can you make instructions foolproof?

In situations like these, when you have to make sense to anybody, it is important to use language which everybody understands. This is when **Standard English** is extremely useful for speakers of English.

LANGUAGE NOTE

You now need to think a bit more about the ways in which people speak differently up and down the country.

Barry Heath's poem was not written in Standard English, so some of you may have found it difficult to understand. That is because it is written in a different *variety* of English.

People in Cornwall sometimes speak a different kind of English from people in Newcastle-upon-Tyne. This means that they have different words, different rules for putting words together and different ways of pronunciation (*accent*). These regional varieties of English are called *dialects*.

Find out any words or combinations of words which are special to where you live. Compare them to the Standard English equivalent.

Standard English is a special dialect which has become important for education, politics, law, TV, radio, newspapers and business. What it means is that sometimes you *need* to use Standard English in order to communicate with other people. The trick is to know *when* it is *appropriate* to use it.

In most of your school work, the teachers use Standard English and expect you to do the same, especially in written work. You should be able to use your own dialects at home and in the playground, and sometimes in school lessons.

Look at the examples of dialects which three girls are talking about to help you further.

Shirley: Now Angela and I want you and the other Angela to have a conversation in, um, the Jamaican creole, not very long, just for a little while, and then repeat it in English afterwards if you can.

Angela 1: Wha' happen Angie? How's things getting on at school, cool?

Angela 2: Yeh, they cool, y'now.

Angela 1: How's you mother?

Angela 2: She alright.

Angela 1: Me see you brother a' home downa Brixton Market de other day y'know, inna record shop.

Angela 2: Me know what him a do down dere 'cause if me mumma catch him she wring him neck fi him y'know.

Shirley: Okay. Thank you. Now could . . .

Angela 1: Alright Angie, later, right?

Angela 2: Yeh, later.

Shirley: Yeh. Could you er . . . repeat that in English please? Find some way to . . .

Angela 2: Right, well she said to me, "Hello . . ."

Shirley: No, I mean I want you to say it, like a conversation a bit like before.

Angela 2: Hello, Angie!

Angela 1: Alright Angie, how are you?

Angela 2: Fine thank you.

Angela 1: I saw your brother in Brixton Market the other day in a record shop.

Angela 2: I don't know what he's doing down there, 'cause if my mother catches him she'll wring his neck for him.

Angela 1: Okay then, I'll see you later, okay?

Angela 2: Yeh, see you.

Angela 1: Bye.

Angela 2: Bye.

Shirley: There we have two different types of dialect, one in Jamaican creole, and one in English.

Angela 1: (*whispering*) Cockney now, Cockney.

Shirley: Um, there's another sort of a dialect, called Cockney, and I wonder if you could repeat that little scene again.

Angela 1: Watcher Ang!

Angela 2: Watcher.

Angela 1: 'Ow yer getting' on at school?

Angela 2: Alright.

Angela 1: 'Ow's yer mum?

Angela 2: She's alright.

Angela 1: I saw your brother in Brixton the other day . . .

Angela 2: Did yer?

Angela 1: . . . I seen him round there, yeh, he was in this record shop.

Angela 2: I dunno what 'e's doing there 'cause if my mum catches 'im she'll wring 'is neck for 'im you know.

Angela 1: Oh yeh?

Angela 2: Yeh.

Angela 1: Alright, Ang, I'll see yer, right?

Angela 2: Yeh, see yer.

Angela 1: Bye.

Angela 2: Yeh, bye.

Angela 1: Give me regards to yer mum, won't yer?

Angela 2: Yeh, same to you love.

Shirley: Right, there . . . (*laughing*) . . . there we have three different dialects.

You could try making a news broadcast in your local dialect, or turn a well-known story into a dialect version.

There will be more about accent, dialect and Standard English in Book 2.

⑨ And here is the news . . .

You hear about terrorist actions, natural disasters and royal babies on the news. But what about your local area? What happens where you live? What makes the news in your town or village? Your next piece of work involves you being news reporters and presenters.

Read, discuss and write

In groups, look through some recent issues of your local newspaper. Collect what you think are the most interesting stories and turn them into a news bulletin for your local radio station. Use tape recorders if you can, or video recorders.

Elect one group to act as editors for the news bulletin. They should check that:

▶ Each group is working on different items or stories.
▶ They know how many words they have to write for each item.
▶ They can decide what they have to explain to their audience of listeners.
▶ They are changing the stories to suit listeners instead of readers.

The writers should remember to:

▶ Choose stories they understand!
▶ Try to find an interesting sequence of stories; decide if sad ones should be first or last, or in the middle. Where should happy stories be?
▶ They need to rewrite the stories so they can be read as news items.
▶ Find some music to open and close the news broadcast.

Village flooded

Police praise rescuers

Royal visit

Gnome thieves hunted

Success for city

Parrot Romeo pines for his Juliet!

DO YOU KNOW WHEN STANDARD ENGLISH OR LOCAL ACCENT/DIALECT IS APPROPRIATE?

10 Girls and boys come out to play!

OK, that is all right for those in year six. But, in year seven, you are becoming grown up. You have been working on making radio bulletins, defusing bombs, trying out your voice.

Here is an important question: Why do boys and girls experience their lives differently?

Read and discuss

Form your groups of boys and girls if you are in a mixed school. Read the extract from Margaret Atwood's novel *Cat's Eye*. She is a Canadian writer who is looking back at her schooldays.

Discuss, in groups, how she writes about the differences between girls and boys at school. Do you have the same kind of experiences? Make a list of activities at school which involve either boys on their own or girls on their own.

I am very curious about the BOYS door. How is going in through a door different if you're a boy? What's in there that merits the strap, just for seeing it? My brother says there's nothing special about the stairs inside, they're plain ordinary stairs. The boys don't have a separate classroom, they're in with us. They go in the BOYS door and end up in the same place we do. I can see the point of the boys' washroom, because they pee differently, and also the boys' yard, because of all the kicking and punching that goes on among them. But the door baffles me. I would like to have a look inside.

Just as there are separate doors for boys and girls, there are also separate parts of the schoolyard. At the front, outside the teachers' entrance, is a dirt field covered with cinders, the boys' playing field. At the side of the school facing away from the street is a hill, with wooden steps going up it and eroded runnels worn down the side, and a few stunted evergreens on top. By custom this is reserved for the girls, and the older ones stand around up there in groups of three or four, their heads bent inwards, whispering, although boys sometimes make charges up the hill, yelling and waving their arms. The cement-paved area outside the BOYS and GIRLS is common territory, since the boys have to cross it in order to go in their door.

Lining up is the only time I see my brother at school. At home we've rigged up a walkie-talkie with two tin cans and a piece of string, which runs between our two bedroom windows and doesn't work very well. We push messages under each other's doors, written in the cryptic language of the aliens, which is filled with x's and z's and must be decoded. We nudge and kick each other under the table, keeping our faces straight above the tablecloth; sometimes we tie our shoe-laces together, for signalling. These are my main communications with my brother now, these raspy tin-can words, sentences without vowels, the Morse of feet.

But in the daytime I lose sight of him as soon as we go out the door. He's up ahead, throwing snowballs; and on the bus he's at the back, in a noisy whirlpool of older boys. After school, after he's gone through the fights that are required of any new boy at any school, he's off helping to wage war on the boys from the Catholic school nearby. It's called Our Lady of Perpetual Help, but the boys from our school have re-named it Our Lady of Perpetual Hell. It's said that the boys from this Catholic school are very tough and that they conceal rocks inside their snowballs.

I know better than to speak to my brother during these times, or to call his or any boy's attention to me. Boys get teased for having younger sisters, or sisters of any kind, or mothers; it's like having new clothes. When he gets anything new my brother dirties it as soon as possible, to avoid having it noticed; and if he has to go anywhere with me and my mother, he walks ahead of us or crosses to the other side of the street. If he's teased about me, he will have to fight some more. For me to contact him, or even to call him by name, would be disloyal. I understand these things, and do my best.

From *Cat's Eye*, Margaret Atwood

Debate

Prepare a debate on this motion:
'Girls should be treated equally with boys at home and at school.'
Enjoy the chance to speak your mind!

Guidelines for holding a debate

► There should be one person to propose the motion first of all.
► There should be one person to oppose the motion after the proposer.
► There should be one person to second the motion.
► There should be one person to second the opposer.
► There should be a chairperson to control the debate.
► Speeches from the floor should follow the four main speakers.
► Each speaker should make sure of what they are going to say, by noting down the points they want to make in their speech.
► A vote on the motion should be taken at the end of the debate.
► Each speaker has a purpose in choosing language carefully – to express a point of view to an audience of classmates.

You have been thinking about speaking and listening as learning activities in this module. You have been keeping a reflective record of your own activities in speaking and listening. Look back at what you have been doing and make some entries in your log which will help you to focus on your successes and problems in the next half term.

11 Telling stories

It is only during the last few hundred years that stories have been written down. Traditionally stories were passed from generation to generation by word of mouth. The first stories which you can remember were probably told to you by your parents or teachers some time before you were able to read stories for yourself. So you can see that the tradition of storytelling is still very much alive.

Just as in writing, it is necessary to consider your **audience** before you begin to tell a story. The tone and the subject matter of the story will vary according to your audience. For the purpose of this exercise we will assume your audience to be your classmates, 11- and 12-year-olds. Your teacher, however, might be able to find you a younger audience. If so, think carefully about how you might vary your story so that it is appropriate for the people you are going to tell it to.

Planning your story

Step 1 Decide what your subject and the setting of the story is. Bear in mind that your audience ought to be familiar with both.

Close your eyes and try to visualise the picture of the scene you imagine.

Step 2 Paint a picture in words. Describe this scene to your partner in as much detail as you can – do not miss anything out. Try to use information provided by all your senses. Do not just describe what you can see; think about the sounds, smells, feelings and tastes too. Do not stop to think – just let your description flow. If you hesitate or stop you might lose the interest of your listener!

Step 3 Having created a picture, now you have to destroy it! Introduce something new which changes the picture completely. Picture the new scene in your mind and follow the same process as you did in Step 2, building the new picture as fully as possible.

Example Your original scene could have featured a forest with its trees, its animals, insects, and people living nearby. Then you could have introduced some men, some bulldozers and the forest being destroyed. Your description of the destruction of the forest could focus on such things as the fleeing animals and the falling trees.

Step 4 Now it is time to turn your descriptions into a real story by introducing a twist of some kind – an event or a series of events. Follow the same process as before.

Example A way of adding a twist to our forest story would be to introduce a rainstorm, which creates a flood, washing away the men and their machines and leaving the way clear for an ending in which the animals return and the forest reclaims the land.

Step 5 To complete your story find an appropriate ending. You might try returning to the original scene.

You could discuss this with your partner, as he or she will already have heard the first four stages and may have some good ideas to help you.

Try out the ending on your partner.

Performing a story

Now put together the five parts and tell the complete story to the other members of your group. You might try telling it to more than one group. Each time you tell your story think about how you might improve it for the next time.

When you are satisfied that your story is as good as it can be, perhaps you might record it or even tell it to the whole class or a different class.

You might like to end this activity by discussing in a small group the differences you found between telling and writing a story. Report your conclusions to the whole class.

1 The reading survey

What do you really read?

Does your mum complain that you do not read enough or are you the type that always has his or her head stuck in a book? Whatever type you are, it is likely that you read a lot more than you think (or your mum thinks) you do.

Research

To help you find out precisely what you do read, keep a log of your reading for two days. From the moment you get up in the morning to the moment you go to sleep at night, list everything – yes, everything – you read in the way shown below.

Introduction

Have you ever looked closely at what you read? Have you looked at the language a writer uses when he or she is writing for you? Have you ever thought why the language used in a teenage magazine is different to the language you meet in your textbooks at school? Have you ever wondered why a letter a friend writes to you looks and sounds so different to the letters you bring home from school? And what about the stories and poems you read? Why do stories and poems work for us? Most of us do not give such questions a thought. This module will help you begin to answer some of these questions.

48 Hours Reading
DAY 1

READING TYPE	WHERE READING TOOK PLACE	REASON FOR READING	TIME SPENT READING
back of Weetabix box	breakfast table	fill time interested in competition	2 mins
warning in bus	on way to school	caught my attention	15 secs
advert	outside cinema	wanted to find out what film was on	10 secs
list of names	assembly in hall	bored, to see if anyone with my name's been school captain	25 secs
Nick's French homework	tutor room	to see if my homework was right	2 mins
The Cartoonist by Betsy Byars	tutor room	enjoying book and wanted to see what would happen to Alfie	5 mins

FIND OUT WHAT YOU _REALLY_ READ WITH THE READING SURVEY.

Presenting the reading survey

When you have completed your reading survey, present to a small group what you have learnt about yourself as a reader. You might find these questions helpful in sorting out what you might say:

▶ What sort of material do you read most?
▶ How much of your reading do you enjoy?
▶ Which type of reading do you most/least enjoy?
▶ What sorts of reasons do you have for reading?
▶ What do you think is the most/least important reading that you do?
▶ When do you do most of your reading?
▶ Where do you do most of your reading?
▶ What is the most interesting/surprising thing you have learnt about your reading habits from doing this survey?

List your 'key' points **briefly** in the order in which you want to make them.

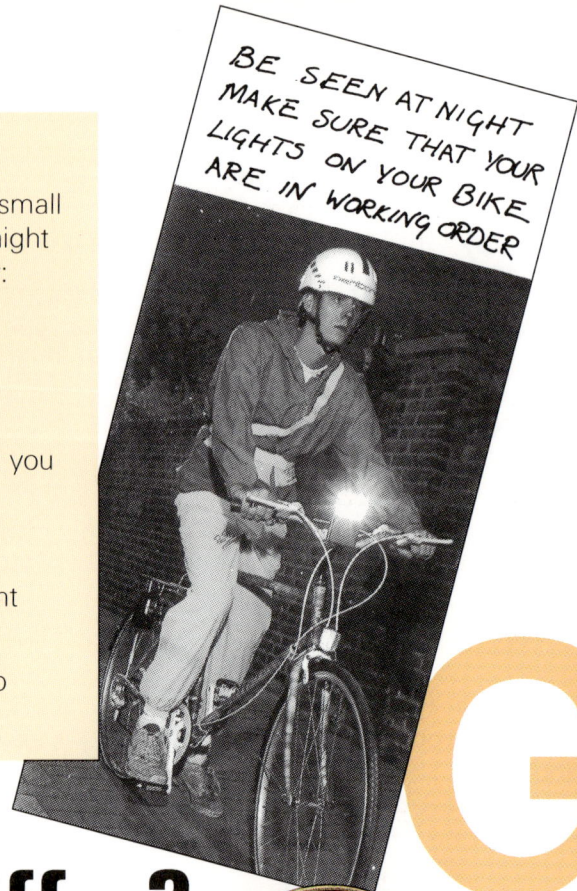

BE SEEN AT NIGHT MAKE SURE THAT YOUR LIGHTS ON YOUR BIKE ARE IN WORKING ORDER

WEST YORKSHIRE POLICE
SAFER CYCLIST

2 How do texts differ?

Spot the difference

By now you have probably realised that you spend a lot more of the day reading than you think. Now let us look in a little more detail at what it is that you read.

We call reading material of any sort **texts**. Here are just some of the typical texts that you might find in a classroom.

Dear Mrs Evans,

> I hope you will excuse Sarah's absence yesterday. She was sick all night and wasn't fit enough to come to school. As she seems better today, I'm sending her to school, but I would appreciate it if you'd keep an eye on her.

> Yours faithfully,

> Yvonne Carter.

Don't write on books

Rhuna Patel

English

IP, Room II, Mrs Evans

PUPILS ARE REMINDED TO PUT THEIR CHAIRS ON THE DESK AT THE END OF THE DAY

LANGUAGE NOTE

We only have to look at these texts to see that they are very different. But how?

There are a number of ways we can look at them. We can ask:

▶ For whom are they written? Or what is their *audience*?

▶ What is their *purpose*? How do the writers of these texts want us to react to them?

▶ How have they been arranged and presented? Or how does their *form* differ?

WOOD GREEN ANIMAL SHELTERS

THIS CAT IS WELL CARED FOR . . . THOUSANDS ARE NOT
PLEASE HELP US TO HELP THEM

Every year thousands of stray and abandoned animals are brought into the Wood Green Animal Shelters. Some have been mis-treated, some injured, others are unwanted for many different reasons. The love and care we give them comes free, the rest costs a great deal of money. Please send a donation to help us give them a future they deserve.

Wood Green Animal Shelters, Highway Cottage, Chishill Road, Heydon, Nr. Royston, Herts. SG8 8NP. Tel: (0763) 838329. Registered Charity No. 298348.

GREENPEACE

This is the story of a boy called Wagstaffe. He was a very ordinary boy in many ways, but he had one big problem – his Mum and Dad. From that big problem all the smaller problems of his life had come. There were millions of them.

Take his name, for instance. Wagstaffe was not his last name – like Smith, or Jones, or Sayeed, say – it was his first, like John, or Simon, or Mohammed. His full name was Wagstaffe Winstanley Watkins Williams. And he hated it.

His Mum and Dad, of course, had ordinary, proper names. His mother was called Wilhelmina (Willie for short) and his father was called Englebert. Wagstaffe could remember how hard they had argued over what to call him. The argument had gone on for so long, in fact, that he was eight before he had been christened. It took four vicars to get him into the font.

Can I borrow your homework? I forgot to do mine last night. Dont let miss see you Pass it under desk

Gazz

Discuss

With a partner try grouping all these different texts in the following ways:

▶ First group all those with the same **audience**.
▶ Then try splitting them up into groups with the same **purpose**.
▶ Finally try splitting them up into groups with a similar **form**.

Did you find any texts difficult to group? Why? What does that tell you about some texts?

Now try looking round your classroom or round a room at home. Find as many different texts as you can and try grouping them in the same way as above.

When you have finished, list your texts by audience, purpose and form.

well as lava and ash, the volcano ...ches out steam and gases. The steam ...mes from water that has seeped ...ough the rocks from the sea or from ...ers. The water boils when it reaches ... magma. Once the steam is blown into ... air, it cools and forms water droplets. ...ere may be so much steam that it ...kes a great rainstorm. When the rain ...xes with the ash that has just fallen, it ...ms a thick black mud.

FIND OUT HOW TEXTS DIFFER BY LOOKING AT THEIR AUDIENCE, PURPOSE AND FORM.

3 Story form 1

Finding the right ingredients

In the last section we found that the texts we read differ. In this section we are going to look at one type of text – the story. This time we will look at the way in which the purpose and audience of the text affects the form of the story.

Discuss

Part 1 is the opening of a story. One of you should read it aloud and the rest should listen carefully.

When you have read Part 1:

You have not heard enough of the story here yet to know what type of story it is. Try now to predict what will happen next if:

▶ this were the beginning of a fairy story
▶ this were the beginning of a detective story
▶ this were the beginning of a ghost story.

Now read on.

Part 2

'There he is,' said Herbert White, as the gate banged loudly and the heavy footsteps came toward the door.

The old man rose with haste and, opening the door, was heard speaking with the new arrival. Mrs White coughed gently as her husband entered the room, followed by a tall, burly man.

'Sergeant-Major Morris,' he said, introducing him.

The sergeant-major shook hands and, taking the seat by the fire, watched contentedly while his host got out whisky and tumblers.

At the third glass his eyes got brighter, and he began to talk. The little family circle regarded with eager interest this visitor from distant parts who spoke of wild scenes and valiant deeds of war and plagues, and strange peoples.

'Twenty-one years of it,' said Mr White, nodding at his wife and son. 'When he went away he was a slip of a youth. Now look at him.'

'He don't look to have taken much harm,' said Mrs White politely.

'I'd like to go to India myself,' said the old man, 'just to look round a bit, you know.'

'Better where you are,' said the sergeant-major shaking his head. He put down the empty glass and, sighing softly, shook it again.

'I should like to see those old temples,' said the old man. 'What was that you started telling me the

Part 1

The night was cold and wet, but in the small parlour the blinds were drawn and the fire burned brightly. Father and son were playing chess. The white-haired old lady was knitting placidly by the fire.

'Listen to the wind,' said Mr White. 'I should hardly think that he'd come tonight.'

Father and son sat with hands poised over the board.

'That's the worst of living so far out,' bawled Mr White, with sudden violence; 'of all the beastly, slushly, out-of-the-way places to live in, this is the worst.'

'Never mind, dear,' said his wife soothingly.

Mr White looked up sharply, and the words died away on his lips.

'And what is there special about it?', inquired Mr

other day about a monkey's paw or something, Morris?'

'Nothing,' said the soldier hastily. 'Leastways nothing worth hearing.'

'Monkey's paw?' said Mrs White curiously.

'Well, it's just a bit of what you might call magic, perhaps,' said the sergeant-major off-handedly.

His three listeners leaned forward eagerly. The visitor absent-mindedly put his empty glass to his lips and then set it down again. His host filled it for him.

'To look at,' said the sergeant-major, fumbling in his pocket, 'it's just an ordinary little paw, dried to a mummy.'

He took something out of his pocket. Mrs White drew back with a grimace, but her son, taking it, examined it curiously.

'And what is there special about it?' inquired Mr White as he took it from his son and, having examined it, placed it upon the table.

'It had a spell put on it by an old fakir,' said the sergeant-major, 'a very holy man. He wanted to show that fate rules people's lives and that those who interfered with it did so to their sorrow. He put a spell on it so that three separate men could each have three wishes from it.'

'Well, why don't you have three, sir?' said Herbert White cleverly.

'I have,' he said quietly, and his blotchy face

HOW DOES THE AUDIENCE AND PURPOSE OF A STORY AFFECT ITS FORM?

whitened. 'And did you really have the three wishes granted?' asked Mrs White.

'I did,' said the sergeant-major, and his glass tapped against his strong teeth.

'And has anybody else wished?' persisted the old lady.

'Yes. The first man had his three wishes. I don't know what the first two were, but the third was for death. That's how I got the paw.'

His tones were so grave that a hush fell upon the group.

'If you've had your three wishes, it's no good to you then, Morris,' said the old man at last. 'What do you keep it for?'

The soldier shook his head. 'Fancy, I suppose,' he said slowly. 'I did have some idea of selling it, but I don't think I will. It has caused enough mischief already. Besides, people won't buy. They think it's a fairy tale, some of them; and those who do think anything of it want to try it first and pay me afterwards.'

'If you could have another three wishes,' said the old man, eyeing him keenly, 'would you have them?'

'I don't know,' said the other. 'I don't know.'

He took the paw and, dangling it between his forefinger and thumb, suddenly threw it upon the fire. White, with a slight cry, stooped down and snatched it off.

'Better let it burn,' said the soldier solemnly.

'If you don't want it, Morris,' said the other, 'give it to me.'

'I won't,' said his friend. 'I threw it on the fire. If you keep it, don't blame me for what happens. Pitch it on the fire again like a sensible man.'

The other shook his head and examined his new possession closely. 'How do you do it?' he asked.

'Hold it up in your right hand and wish aloud,' said the sergeant-major, 'but I warn you.'

'Sounds like the *Arabian Nights*,' said Mrs White, as she rose and began to set the supper. 'Don't you think you might wish for four pairs of hands for me?'

Her husband drew the paw from his pocket, and then all three burst into laughter as the sergeant-major, with a look of alarm on his face, caught him by the arm.

'If you must wish,' he said gruffly, 'wish for something sensible.'

Mr White dropped it back in his pocket and motioned his friend to the table. During supper the paw was partly forgotten, and afterwards the three sat listening to more of the soldier's adventures in India.

'If the tale about the monkey's paw is not more truthful than those he has been telling us,' said Herbert, as the door closed behind their guest, 'we shan't make much out of it.'

'Did you give him anything for it, father?' asked Mrs White looking at her husband closely.

'A trifle,' he said. 'He didn't want it, but I made him take it. And he begged me again to throw it away.'

'Likely,' said Herbert, with pretended horror. 'Why, we're going to be rich and famous and happy. Wish to be an emperor, father, to begin with; then you can't be henpecked.'

Mr White took the paw from his pocket and eyed it doubtfully. 'I don't know what to wish for, and that's a fact,' he said slowly. 'It seems to me I've got all I want.'

'If only the house was paid for, you'd be quite happy, wouldn't you!' said Herbert, with his hand on his shoulder. 'Well, wish for two hundred pounds, then; that'll just do it.'

His father, smiling, held up the paw. His son winked at his mother, sat down at the piano, and struck a few impressive chords.

'I wish for two hundred pounds,' said the old man distinctly.

A fine crash from the piano greeted the words, interrupted by a shuddering cry from the old man. His wife and son ran toward him.

'It moved,' he cried, with a glance of disgust at the object as it lay on the floor. 'As I wished, it twisted in my hand like a snake.'

'Well, I don't see the money,' said his son, as he picked it up and placed it on the table, 'and I bet I never shall.'

'It must have been your imagination,' said his wife.

He shook his head. 'Never mind, though; there's no harm done, but it gave me a shock all the same.'

They sat down by the fire again. Outside, the wind was higher than ever, and the old man jumped nervously at the sound of a door banging upstairs. A silence, unusual and depressing, settled upon all three, which lasted until the old couple arose to retire for the night.

'I expect you'll find the cash tied up in a big bag in the middle of your bed,' said Herbert, as he bade them goodnight, 'and something horrible sitting up on top of the dresser watching you as you pocket your ill-gotten gains.'

He sat alone in the darkness, gazing at the dying fire and seeing faces in it. The last face was so horrible that he gazed at it in amazement. It got so vivid that, with a little uneasy laugh, he felt on the table for a glass containing a little water to throw over it. His hand grasped the monkey's paw, and with a little shiver he wiped his hand on his coat and went up to bed.

Which type of story is it? A fairy story? A detective story? A ghost story?

Write

Copy the grid below and use it to list the clues that told you what sort of story it is.

CHARACTERS	SETTING	EVENTS	LANGUAGE

Discuss

Before you read the last section, compare your grid to your partner's. See if you can list any other ingredient of a typical ghost story.

Now discuss the following:
▶ What do you think is the purpose of a ghost story like this one?
▶ For whom do you think this story is written?

Now use the same grid to plan a very different sort of ghost story.
▶ One of you should plan the ingredients for a ghost story for young children,
▶ the other should plan a ghost story which sets out to make the reader laugh.

When you have finished, show each other your grids. How do they differ from the grid you made for a typical ghost story?

Read and discuss

Before you return to the story, try to predict how you think the story will end.

Use your knowledge of what typical ghost stories consist of and the clues you might have picked up in the first two episodes.

Write

Try writing the end of this story. Use what you have learnt during this unit. You can either:
▶ write the ending that you think should follow from what you have read,
▶ write an ending which will make the reader laugh, or
▶ write an ending that you think much younger children would like to read.

Read

Now finish reading the story. How does it compare with your ending?

Part 3

In the brightness of the wintry sun next morning as it streamed over the breakfast table, he laughed at his fears.

'I suppose all old soldiers are the same,' said Mrs White. 'The idea of our listening to such nonsense! How could wishes be granted in these days? And if they could, how could two hundred pounds hurt you, father?'

'Might drop on his head from the sky,' said Herbert jokingly.

'Morris said the things happened so naturally,' said his father, 'that you might think it was only coincidence.'

'Well, don't break into the money before I come back,' said Herbert as he rose from the table. 'I'm afraid it'll turn you into a mean, greedy man, and we shall have to disown you.'

His mother laughed and, following him to the door, watched him down the road.

'Herbert will have some more of his funny remarks, I expect, when he comes home,' she said.

'I dare say,' said Mr White, 'but for all that, the thing moved in my hand; that I'll swear to.'

'You thought it did,' said the old lady soothingly.

'I *say* it did,' replied the other. 'There was no thought about it.'

His wife made no reply.

In the late afternoon Mrs White was watching the mysterious movements of a man outside, who, peering in an undecided fashion at the house, appeared to be trying to make up his mind to enter. In thinking about the two hundred pounds, she noticed that the stranger was well dressed. Three times he paused at the gate, and then walked on again. The fourth time he stood with his hand upon it, and then suddenly flung it open and walked up the path. Mrs White went to the door and brought the stranger, who seemed ill at ease, into the room. He gazed at her, and listened in a preoccupied fashion as the old lady apologized for the appearance of the room. She then waited as patiently as she could for him to state his business, but he was at first strangely silent.

'I – was asked to call,' he said at last. 'I come from Maw and Meggins.'

The old lady started. 'Is anything the matter?' she asked breathlessly. 'Has anything happened to Herbert? What is it? What is it?'

Her husband interrupted. 'There, there, mother,' he said hastily. 'Sit down, and don't jump to conclusions. You've not brought bad news, I'm sure, sir.'

'I'm sorry –' began the visitor.

'Is he hurt?' demanded the mother wildly.

The visitor bowed in assent. 'Badly hurt,' he said quietly, 'but he is not in any pain.'

'Oh, thank God!' said the old woman clasping her hands. 'Thank God for that! Thank –'

She broke off suddenly as the sinister meaning of his words dawned upon her. She caught her breath

and turning to her slower-witted husband, laid a trembling old hand upon his. There was a long silence.

'He was caught in the machinery,' said the visitor in a low voice.

'Caught in the machinery,' repeated Mr White, in a dazed fashion.

He sat staring blankly out at the window and took his wife's hand into his own.

'He was the only one left to us,' he said, turning gently to the visitor. 'It is hard.'

The other coughed and, rising, walked slowly to the window. 'The firm wished me to convey their sincere sympathy to you in your great loss,' he said, without looking round.

There was no reply. The old woman's face was white, her eyes staring.

'I am to say that Maw and Meggins disclaim all responsibility,' continued the other. 'They admit no liability at all, but in consideration of your son's services, they wish to present you with a certain sum as compensation.'

Mr White dropped his wife's hand and, rising to his feet, gazed with a look of horror at his visitor.

His dry lips shaped the words, 'How much?'

'Two hundred pounds,' was the answer.

Unconscious of his wife's shriek, the old man smiled faintly, put out his hands like a sightless man, and dropped, a senseless heap, to the floor.

In the huge new cemetery, some two miles distant, the old people buried their dead and came back to the house steeped in shadow and silence. It was all over so quickly that at first they could hardly realize it. Sometimes they hardly exchanged a word, for now they had nothing to talk about, and their days were long and weary.

It was about a week after that the old man, waking suddenly in the night, stretched out his hand and found himself alone. The room was in darkness, and the sound of weeping came from the window. He raised himself in bed and listened.

'Come back,' he said tenderly. 'You will be cold.'

'It is colder for my son,' said the old woman, and she wept afresh.

The sound of her sobs died away on his ears. The bed was warm, and his eyes heavy with sleep. He slept until a sudden wild cry from his wife awoke him with a start.

'The paw!' she cried wildly. 'The monkey's paw!'

He started up in alarm. 'Where? Where is it? What's the matter?'

She came stumbling across the room toward him. 'I want it,' she said quietly. 'You've not destroyed it?'

'It's in the parlour,' he replied. 'Why?'

'I only just thought of it,' she said hysterically. 'Why didn't I think of it before? Why didn't *you* think of it?'

'Think of what?' he questioned.

'The other two wishes,' she replied rapidly. 'We've had one.'

'Was not that enough?' he demanded fiercely.

'No,' she cried, 'we'll have one more. Go down and get it quickly, and wish our boy alive again.'

The man sat up in bed and flung the covers off. 'Good God, you are mad!' he cried, aghast.

'Get it,' she panted; 'get it quickly, and wish – Oh, my boy, my boy!'

Her husband struck a match and lit the candle. 'Get back to bed,' he said unsteadily. 'You don't know what you are saying.'

'We had the first wish granted,' said the old woman feverishly. 'Why not the second?'

'A coincidence,' stammered the old man.

'Go and get it and wish,' cried his wife, quivering with excitement.

The old man's voice shook. 'He has been dead ten days, and besides he – I would not tell you else, but – I could only recognize him by his clothing. If he was too terrible for you to see then, how now?'

'Bring him back,' cried the old woman and dragged him toward the door. 'Do you think I fear my own child?'

He went down in the darkness, and felt his way to the parlour. The paw was in its place. A horrible fear that the unspoken wish might bring his mutilated son before him sooner than he could escape from the room seized upon him, and he caught his breath as he found that he had lost the direction of the door. His brow cold with sweat, he felt his way round the table and groped along the wall until he found himself in the small passage with the ugly thing in his hand.

Even his wife's face seemed changed as he entered the room. It was white and he was afraid of her.

'Wish!' she cried, in a strong voice.

'It is foolish and wicked,' he said.

'Wish!' repeated his wife.

He raised his hand. 'I wish my son alive again.'

The paw fell to the floor, and he looked at it fearfully. Then he sank trembling into a chair as the old woman, with burning eyes, walked to the window and raised the blind.

He sat until he was chilled with the cold, glancing occasionally at the figure of the old woman peering through the window. The old man, with an unspeakable sense of relief at the failure of the paw, crept back to his bed, and a minute or two afterward the old woman came to his side.

Neither spoke, but listened silently to the ticking of the clock. A stair creaked, and a squeaky mouse scurried noisily through the wall. The darkness was heavy, and after lying for some time gathering up his courage, he took the box of matches and, striking one, went downstairs for a candle.

At the foot of the stairs, the match went out, and he paused to strike another. At the same moment a knock, so quiet as to be scarcely audible, sounded on the front door.

The matches fell from his hand and spilled in the passage. He stood motionless, his breath suspended until the knock was repeated. Then he turned and fled swiftly back to his room and closed the door behind him. A third knock sounded through the house.

'What's that?' cried the old woman, starting up.

'A rat,' said the old man in shaking tones – 'a rat. It passed me on the stairs.'

His wife sat up in bed listening. A loud knock resounded through the house.

'It's Herbert!' she screamed. 'It's Herbert!'

She ran to the door, but her husband was before her and, catching her by the arm, held her tightly.

'What are you going to do?' he whispered hoarsely.

'It's my boy; it's Herbert!' she cried, struggling. 'I forgot it was two miles away. What are you holding me for? Let go. I must open the door.'

'For God's sake, don't let it in,' cried the old man, trembling.

'You're afraid of your own son,' she cried struggling. 'Let me go. I'm coming, Herbert; I'm coming!'

There was another knock, and another. The old woman with a sudden wrench broke free and ran from the room. Her husband followed to the landing and called after her as she hurried downstairs. He heard the chain rattle back and the bottom bolt drawn slowly and stiffly from the socket. Then the old woman's voice, strained and panting:

'The bolt,' she cried loudly. 'Come down. I can't reach it.'

But her husband was on his hands and knees groping wildly on the floor in search of the paw. If he could only find it before the thing outside got in. The knocks echoed through the house, and he heard the scraping of a chair as his wife put it down in the passage against the door. He heard the creaking of the bolt as it came slowly back, and at the same moment he found the monkey's paw, and frantically breathed his third and last wish.

The knocking ceased suddenly, although the echoes of it were still in the house. He heard the chair drawn back, and the door opened. A cold wind rushed up the staircase. A long, loud wail of disappointment and misery from his wife gave him courage to run down to her side, and then to the gate beyond. The street lamp shone on a quiet and deserted road.

The Monkey's Paw, W.W. Jacobs

4 Story form 2

Putting the ingredients in order

We have seen how the ingredients in a story are affected by the audience the writer is writing for and by what effect he wants his story to have. The ingredients of a story, however, are only part of the form of a story. These ingredients have to be put in an order that will involve the reader and make him or her want to read on. This order is an important aspect of the form of a story, yet in most stories it remains remarkably similar despite the purpose and audience of the story.

LANGUAGE NOTE

Most stories have three parts:

▶ *Part 1: Setting the scene* The first part introduces us to some of the people in the story, the situation they find themselves in and the place or time the story is set in.
▶ *Part 2: The action* In the middle section of the story something happens to at least one of the characters we have met in Part 1.
▶ *Part 3: The result* The story finishes by showing us the result of what happened in Part 2.

Read and discuss

Here is a simple modern fairy tale written by a pupil. As you can see it is exploded on the page. Put it back together in an order which makes sense.

In order to complete this exercise you will have to think about the different parts of a story.
▶ First, collect all the sentences that seem to 'set the scene' and then put them in an order that makes sense.
▶ Then, collect the sentences that deal with what happens to one of the characters that you have met in the first section. Again put them in order.
▶ Finally, collect the sentences that describe the result of the event dealt with in the second section.

When you have finished, read the story through. Does it make sense?

This witch was a bad witch and because she was so angry at not having been invited to the christening she decreed that at the age of 16 years the little princess would prick her finger and sleep for 100 years.

MORAL: Let sleeping princesses lie.

Once upon a time, many years ago, there lived a King and Queen who reigned over a foreign land. After a few years of marriage they had a daughter whom they called Hilda.

After several hours the prince, whose name was Bertram, managed to get through the undergrowth and a few moments later he found the princess. He kissed her softly.

He was rather a grotty prince with a wooden leg, false teeth, a glass eye, acne and BO, but he *was* a prince. By now the castle had been overrun by large bushes.

It was 16 years later and the princess was walking through the castle, hopefully kissing frogs, when she came upon a room she'd never seen before.

She decided to try it out, but having always bought her clothes from Marks & Spencer she did not know how to sew, and consequently pricked her finger. She instantly fell asleep as did everyone else in the castle.

'You stupid idiot!' She yelled. 'I was just having a snooze.' And she threw him out of the window.

To her christening ceremony were invited all the witches and fairies in those parts. All, that is, except one.

It was 100 years later when the prince arrived at the castle.

On entering it she discovered a brand new Singer electronic programmable sewing machine with twin VU meters and an automatic silencer.

by Sean Lowde

HOW DO YOU ORDER THE INGREDIENTS OF A STORY?

Changing the ingredients

In the last unit we saw how writers choose their ingredients according to their purpose and audience.

What do you think the writer of this story's purpose was? List the ingredients that help him achieve the reaction he wants from the reader.

Whom do you think he is writing this story for? List the ingredients that show you what sort of reader he had in mind.

5 Poetry form 1

Rhythm and rhyme

Poems, like stories, have forms that are affected by audience and purpose. In fact, some of the most recognisable forms you come across when you are reading are found in poems. As you read, you tune into the forms even though you may not recognise them! But if the form does not match the audience or purpose you certainly know it.

Read and discuss

In this poem the poet is still working on its form. He wants to add another verse in the space. He has written three final verses. Discuss with a partner which of the three best fits the purpose of the poem in your opinion.

WHY DO POEMS SOUND DIFFERENT TO STORIES?

Best Friends

It's Susan I talk to not Tracey,
Before that I sat next to Jane;
I used to be best friends with Lynda
But these days I think she's a pain.

Natasha's all right in small doses
I meet Mandy sometimes in town;
I'm jealous of Annabel's pony
And I don't like Nicola's frown.

I used to go skating with Catherine,
Before that I went there with Ruth;
And Kate's so much better at trampoline:
She's a showoff, to tell you the truth.

I think I'm going off Susan,
She borrowed my comb yesterday;
I think I might sit next to Tracey,
She's nearly my best friend: she's OK.

I think I'm going off Susan Higgs,
She's always knicking my pen;
I'll sit next to Tracey Hill instead.
She's my best friend now, OK?

I think I'm going off Susan now;
She copied my work in French.
I want to sit next to Janey Price;
She's my best friend now, OK?

Adrian Henri

How did you make up your mind when deciding which of the three possible verses seemed to fit best? Did you listen to the sound of the poem? Did one verse seem to sound better than the others?

LANGUAGE NOTE

When you were making up your mind about which verse sounded best you were probably influenced by the sound of the poem. The poet has arranged the words he has chosen in certain patterns.

These patterns help create a *rhythm* or 'beat' to the lines. If you read the poem aloud you should be able to hear this beat.

You will also probably have been influenced by the *rhyme* at the end of each line. Again if you look carefully you can see that the second and fourth lines of each verse rhyme or end in the same sound. So the rhyme-scheme is: a b a b.

Write and discuss

Try rewriting the first two verses of 'Best Friends' so that they mean the same but they lose their rhythm and rhyme.

Now try reading them aloud. What has happened to the effect of the 'poem' now?

Read and discuss

Try finishing this incomplete poem, 'In the Playground'. In order to do this, you will have to discuss the purpose of the first part of the poem and try to pick out the rhythm that is set up in the second and third verses.

In the Playground

**In the playground
at the back of our house
there have been some changes.**

**They said the climbing frame was
NOT SAFE
so they sawed it down.**

**They said the paddling pool was
NOT SAFE
so they drained it dry.**

**They said . . . .
. . . .
They said . . . .
. . . .
. . . .
They said . . . .
. . . .
. . . .**

**Sawn down
drained dry
taken away
fenced in
locked up.**

**How do you feel?
Safe?**

Michael Rosen

Now one of you should try reading your poem aloud? Why do you think the rhythm of the poem is so important in the second to sixth verses?

⑥ Poetry form 2

Finding an order

We saw, when we looked at stories, that even though the ingredients in stories may change according to audience and purpose, the sequence of the parts of a story remain basically the same.

The order of the ingredients of a poem is much more the choice of the individual poet and largely depends upon the purpose of the poem.

Discuss

Here are three versions of a poem by Adrian Henri called 'Africa'. They are basically the same poem. The main difference is that the lines have been put in a different order.

What do you think the writer's purpose was in writing this poem? How does he want us to react?

Which do you think is the most effective version and which do you think is the least effective? Try to explain your decision by referring to the order of the lines.

I suddenly thought
Of the faces I see on TV
Of the children of Africa
Stomachs full of emptiness
Little legs like sugarcanes
Swarms of flies round big sad eyes
As I asked for another piece of cake.

———————

I asked for another piece of cake
And suddenly thought
Of the faces I see on TV
Of the children of Africa
Stomachs full of emptiness
Little legs like sugarcanes
Swarms of flies round big sad eyes.

———————

I asked for another piece of cake
And suddenly thought
Of the children of Africa
Of Swarms of flies round big sad eyes
Of little legs like sugarcanes
Of stomachs full of emptiness
Of their faces that I see on TV.

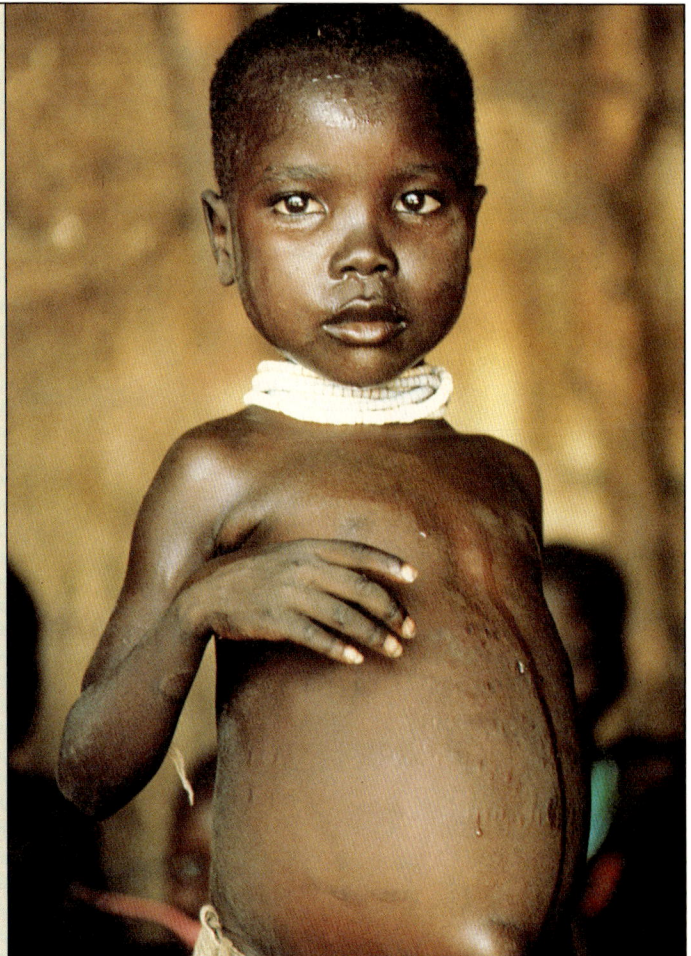

In the last exercise we saw how the order of the lines in a poem can affect the effectiveness of the poem. The poet has to try to find the right order for his purpose.

However, poets often write in verses, or groups of lines. On p. 34, the poet Wes Magee has written in two-line verses, but the printer has made two serious mistakes. Can you spot what they are?

HOW DO POETS ORDER THE INGREDIENTS OF THEIR POEMS?

Read and reflect

Week of Winter Weather

On Monday icy rain poured down
and flooded drains all over town.

Christmas Eve was Sunday and
snow fell like foam across the land.

Friday's frost that bit your ears
was cold enough to freeze your tears.

On Wednesday bursts of hail and sleet;
no-one walked along our street.

Thursday stood out clear and calm
but the sun was paler than my arm.

Saturday's sky was ghostly grey;
we smashed ice on the lake today.

Wes Magee

What do you think the poet's purpose was?
How did the printer's mistake spoil the poem?

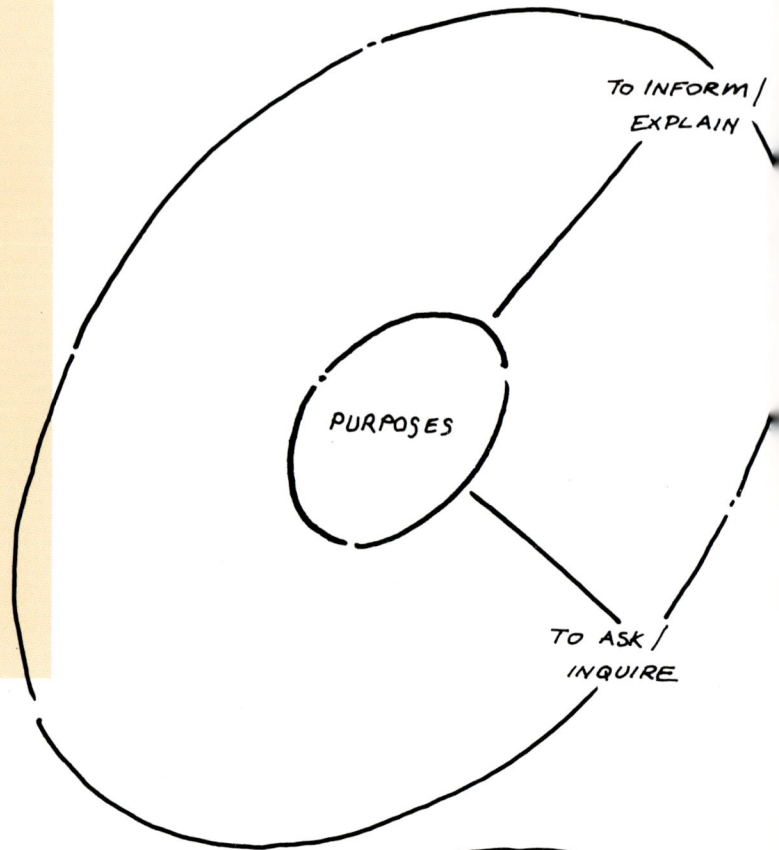

7 Letters: types and styles

Private and public

Now let us look at a different
type of writing – letters – and see
how the audience and purpose
not only affects the way the
letter is organised but also
affects the language, or **style**,
that the writer uses.

Brainstorm

Take two large pieces of paper
and produce spidergrams,
like the ones shown here, to
list all the purposes people
have for writing letters and all
the types of different audience
for letters you can think of.

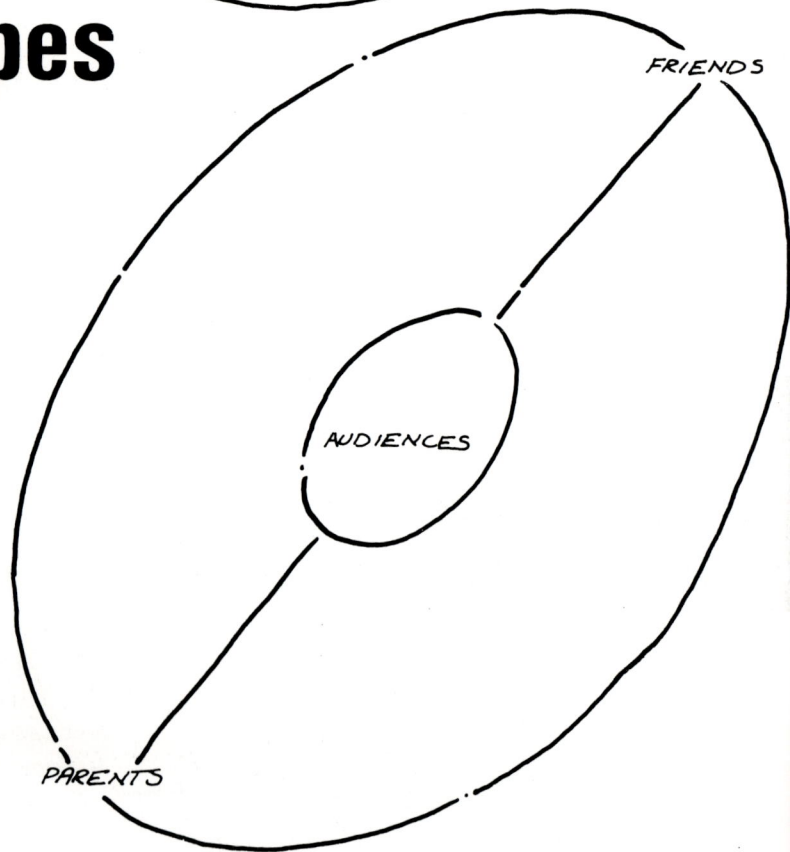

TO INFORM /
EXPLAIN

PURPOSES

TO ASK /
INQUIRE

FRIENDS

AUDIENCES

PARENTS

HOW DOES AUDIENCE AND PURPOSE AFFECT THE LETTERS YOU READ?

Read and discuss

Here is a range of letters that you might have referred to in your reading log and on p. 23. Each letter is numbered. Read each letter and decide amongst yourselves:

▶ the type of **audience** the letter is written for
▶ the **purpose** or purposes of the letter.

When you come to an agreement, record the number of the letter against the appropriate purpose and audience descriptions on your spidergrams.

Try to collect your own examples of letters which have been written for similar reasons and for similar audiences. Number them and add them to the spidergrams. (Check with your parents first that you can use them.)

1

LIVINGSTONE COMPREHENSIVE SCHOOL
KNIGHTS ROAD
EVESBURY

Head: Mrs E. Carter
Deputy Heads: Mr A. Jones
Mrs L. Price

8 June 1990

Dear Parent

I regret to inform you that the school will be closed from 10 to 17 June to facilitate major repairs to the buildings following the recent storm damage. Staff will be setting pupils work to be undertaken at home during this period and would appreciate parental support in ensuring that it is completed.

Yours faithfully

E. Carter
Head

2

No milk till further notice for No. 3

3

Animal rights

ON READING the letter submitted by S Mortimer, on 19 April, I would like to point out something to the 'animal lover' and others like him.

Animals should not have as many rights as humans, simply because mankind is the dominant race. Animals could not handle our rights – can they vote, write, communicate with humans? Are animals such as vicious dogs responsible? No!

I doubt that S Mortimer understands the meaning of 'ill-treated animals'. This could be swatting a fly or killing a couple of hundred bacteria by scratching yourself.

Neil McGinty, 15

4

Dear Jo,

I have funny dreams which speed up faster and faster until I wake up screaming and crying then I find myself in my mum and dad's room. I go there automatically. They ask me what the dream was about and I don't know. I can't remember, but it only just happened! All I know is that it is frightening. My friend had a dream where it sped up and he said he was petrified. What are causing these dreams? PS: I have them regularly.

5

St. Anne's Hotel
Kenton
York

16th June 1990

Hi Kate,

How's school? We're having an ace time up here. I thought it would be a real drag with just me, mum and dad, but (faint! faint!) it's great. There's so much to do. We went to a place called the Yorrick Centre. You go on a sort of train which takes you through this model Viking village. There's smells, noises everything, I'll tell you about it when we get back.

See you.

Love
Wendy

Once you have gathered a collection of letters and sorted them out in the way described, try to compare the letters which have been written for similar purposes and audiences. Look at:

▶ the way the letters have been set out
▶ how the reader is referred to at the start of the letter
▶ the sort of language that has been used
▶ the way the writer has signed off at the end.

Improvise

Take letter 1 from the collection of letters above and rewrite it, using the language and layout a teenager might use writing a letter to a close friend.

Improvise the scene in which one of you hands over this letter to your parents. Try to imagine how they might react, particularly if it was handwritten.

Use these questions to help you get inside the scene:
▶ What might the parents think about the letter?
▶ What conclusions might they draw about the person who wrote it?
▶ How does the letter differ from what they might expect?

▶ How might the pupil explain the way the letter has been written?

Try repeating the scene but changing roles.

When you are happy that you created a scene with some realistic reactions, discuss the following questions:
▶ What have you learnt about the way people write letters?
▶ Why do letters differ in layout, language and organisation?
▶ What happens if people use different language in letters to the language you expect them to use?

⑧ Language for a young audience

Your language?

When we receive letters, the language the writer has used will depend upon how well he or she knows us and why he or she is writing. Much of the reading you do will be of texts which have been specially written for you. The writer will have tried to choose words that you can understand and relate to, yet still help to have the effect upon you he or she wants.

Read and write

Here is a passage from a popular magazine aimed at your age group. Some of the words have been missed out. What do you think they are?

I Belong to Glasgow

Oh, 'Glesga toon'! Believe it or not readers, but just take one guess at who spent _____ in Scotland's city o' culture? None other than Matt Dillon!! Yep, Mr Moodsome and his younger _____, Kevin, were the guest of Scottish 'beefcake' Sean O'Kane (remember that _____ from 'The Interceptor'?) over the festive season! It seems Sean – who's big in _____ – is best _____ with the Dillons, so he invited them o'er to pull the turkey and eat the crackers, etc. Plus, he took them to see The Waterboys on Hogmanay! Yo! Crazy! 'Rad'!

Look at p. 136 for the words the writers used.

WHAT SORT OF LANGUAGE DO WRITERS USE WHEN WRITING FOR YOU?

Now go back to the passage and list any other words and phrases that seem to be aimed at a young teenage audience.

Discuss and research

Look carefully at the passage. How many of these 'teenage words and phrases' do you really use?

Try brainstorming to produce a list of words and phrases that you do use, which adults or young children are unlikely to.

LANGUAGE NOTE

What we have been calling 'teenage words' are part of a teenage *register*. Registers are types of language used by groups of people. To be a part of that group, you should know the words and phrases that make up that register which only that group uses.

Write

Try writing a newsletter for the pupils in your year made up of newsy items like the one you have studied, but about the things that are going on in the school which they might be interested in.

Make it clear that this newsletter is specifically written for them by using your knowledge of teenage register.

⑨ Reasons for writing

Why write at all?

We have seen so far that what we read is very varied in audience, form and style. The way a piece of writing is organised and the language used depend upon who is going to read it.

Yet we have also suggested that it is not the only thing affecting the way something is written. This exercise will also help you look more closely at the different **purposes** for writing.

The story 'The Fall' that you are about to read (here and on p. 38) is made up of different types of reading material.

You will notice that it has been printed in the wrong order. In your group, sort it out so that it tells a story.

MaX

FEATURES RaP'S HOTTEST

CHIP'n'THE C

7.30p.m.SATUR

15 FEBRUARY

SUPPORTED BY

the SCRATCH

FAN FALLS FIFTY FEET

A schoolboy rap fan is recovering in hospital after a fifty foot fall. Jon Clark, 12, broke both legs falling from the top storey of Nelson Mandela flats, Firwood. Rap fan, Jon, had been banned from attending the Chip 'N' Max's Cookies Concert at Firwood. Trying to get out of his family's fifth storey flat, Jon slipped and fell fifty feet. Fortunately a tree partially broke his fall. Mr and Mrs Clark were unavailable for comment.

WHAT DO PEOPLE WRITE TO US?

FEBRUARY 1990

15 SATURDAY

The old man's grounded me !.!!!
One look at my report and that
was it. He blew his top. He snatched
me ear-phones off me and threw
them in the bin and started
giving me an ear-full of how I
should buck my ideas up, empty
my head of this rapping rubbish
and start working at school. Well,
if he thinks he can make me
give up rapping he can forget
it. He can't make me and he
can't ground me either. I'm
going to Max's tonight
whether he likes it or not.

RICHARD — JON SAYS SEE YOU AT MAX'S AT 7.00. DINNER'S IN FRIDGE. PUT IN MICROWAVE FOR 2 MINS. BE HOME BY 10.30. OR ELSE !

Firwood High School
Tutor's Comments:

Name. J. Clark...

Tutor Group. I H..

Jon's behaviour at school recently has
been giving real cause for concern.
Though he is obviously an able boy, he
is under-achieving and a number of his
subject teachers in this report remark
upon his lack of concentration during
lessons. He seems to be able to think
of nothing but 'rap music'. Whilst it
is encouraging to note that something
at least can engage Jon's interest, he
must find time to devote to his school
work.

Tutor. S. Lucas...............

Head of Year's Comments:
I endorse what Ms Lucas has written above.

Head of year. R. Lowe:...............

To
The birdman of Firwood
We've heard your news
N' are sad to hear
Of your bad luck
But dont shed a tear
Your legs'll soon mend
'N' you'll be back at shool
So keep on smilin'
And just stay cool !!!!

From
The rappers of I H

Perform

Now, as a group, divide up 'The Fall' so that each of you has at least one different type of writing. You are going to record this story for another group. To do this successfully you will have to find the right 'voice'.

It helps to think about the reason the writer had for writing. Is he angry and wants to get something off his chest? Is he trying to persuade the reader to do something? Is he just giving information? Is he warning? Or does he have some other reason?

Once you have decided on the reason for writing, try to make your voice sound right. Try to match it to the writer's reason for writing and practise reading the piece.

Rikki
Wanna go to Max's
tonight, Chip 'n' the
Cookies are playing.
I haven't seen them
before but Steve Daker
says they're ace and he
should know, shouldn't he?
The old man's given me some
extra dosh for helping him
fix the car, so if you're
short I can lend you some.
If I don't see you at school
tomorrow I'll give you a bell.

Jon

Discuss

Once each of you is happy with your reading, as a group try performing the story aloud. Discuss the results amongst yourselves.

▶ Did each piece sound right?
▶ Could you hear the difference between the different types of writing?
▶ Did any pieces sound similar? If so, why was that the case?
▶ What made some of the pieces sound different?

MODULE 3 WRITING

What do you write?

Introduction

In this module you will be exploring some ideas about the process of writing. First you will be looking at writing both at home and at school, then you will be focusing closely on the writing of stories. By the end of this module you will know more about the writing process and the craft of writing stories. In Module 6: Writing you will be exploring varieties of writing such as poetry, diaries, letters, autobiographies and stories which use several different kinds of writing.

To help with your development as a writer, in all subjects at school, not only English, you can log your writing, noting down your successes and problems.

1 The writing survey

Well, what did you write last week?

Record and discuss

Under each day list the writing you did; on some days you may have nothing to put in; do not worry about that.

SUNDAY	MONDAY	TUESDAY	WEDNESDAY	THURSDAY	FRIDAY	SATURDAY

Compare your lists with a partner. Add anything new which he or she has to your list. Then, in groups, pick out the writing which you do at home and the writing you do at school.

Do you write more at home or at school? Ask your teacher to help the class to make two charts; head one **Class Writing – At Home**, head the other **Class Writing – At School**.

For each day of the week fill in the class charts. What differences do you notice between the Home chart and the School chart?

Compare your results with the survey on p. 40 from a secondary school.

If you are not yet a published author, you will very probably write much more at school than you do at home.

HAVE A CLOSE LOOK AT **WHAT** YOU WRITE, **WHEN** AND **WHY**.

A Writing Survey

Activities undertaken by both pupils and adults	By pupils	By adults
Charts/diagrams	27	2
Birthday cards	12	4
Personal letters	11	14
Essays	33	3
Business letters	1	12
Informal notes	3	6
Log book entries	105	20
Notes	61	6
Form filling	3	33
Bingo	7	45
Football pools	1	9
Telephone messages	2	9
Marked exercises	20	1
Crossword	22	39
Competitions/puzzles	4	9
Appointments	2	9
Shopping lists	1	13
Paying-in slips	1	4
Typing	12	14
Mail-order documents	3	2

Activities undertaken by one group only

By pupils only		By adults only	
Doodling	2	Cheques	17
Worksheets	45	Envelopes	10
Answering questions	58	Pension books	4
Writing on the board	1	Accounts	14
Labelling	1	Betting slips	4
Signing name	3	Scoring sheets	10
		Telephone notes	9
		Pay queries	3
		Reports	6
		Surveys	3
		Clock-cards	2
		Invoices	14
		Memos	2
		References	4
		Bank communications	13

Why do you write at school?

Discuss

In groups, discuss some of the reasons for writing, in all your subjects. Focus on the following questions:
▶ Is writing sometimes fun? If it is, when? What sort of writing is it?
▶ What do we learn through writing?
▶ What writing do we do in different subjects?
▶ Do we do the same sorts of writing in different subjects?
▶ What problems do we have with writing?
▶ What do we need to know to help us write?

Writing helps you to learn, about yourself, about school subjects and about the world outside school. It has a lot of parts, like a car. As you work in school you will find out more about these. To start with, we shall focus on stories, because you all can write them. So you should feel at home with this module.

Project: record and reflect

To keep your progress as a writer in focus you can keep a writer's log.

You need:

▶ a book to write in or blank grids from your teacher
▶ a favourite pen or pencil
▶ thinking time
▶ writing time
▶ help from your teachers to get you started and keep you going.

You need to know:

▶ the log is for **you** to think about your writing
▶ the log is different from a diary: a diary often has very personal and private thoughts written down in it; your log will have thoughts about your writing in it, which you will want to discuss with your teachers regularly
▶ you can write down your thoughts about writing in all your subjects, not only English
▶ the log will not be marked or graded
▶ you can use the log to help to identify your successes and your problems as a writer
▶ you can compare your log with friends' logs
▶ you can keep some pages for words you find difficult to spell
▶ you can keep some pages for keeping notes on punctuation.

Here are some examples of log entries for writing in maths made by some primary school children. You could use these to start you thinking for your own log entries.

Until today, I thought that multiplying fractions was easy. Now I realize it isn't. God help me when I do algebra!

When I first came to school this morning, I was cold. But as the morning went on, I got warmer this helped me to do maths. I was glad when playtime came.

I would also want to know If you mark our work like this my capabilitys or my speed or my neatness or all of them. I also got stuck when I have to simplifie before multiplying fractions.

I Don't understand Fractions very well and I Don't understand hg's and g's at ; all please could you help me I am also not very good at English

I knew I got the right answer because we had to go through it 25 times This was boring I kept dropping my coin when I was tossing it and Mr H told me off. It wasnt my fault How was I to know I can't toss coins?

14.1.87

why didn't you come out —
that's why I'm there

I was afraid you'd say "you should know that by now!"

This morning we did fractions, well I did anyway! I didn't want to go out to Mrs Rosenfelt for help, so I just set and tried to work it out myself I couldn't understand

I have troble with some of the large numbers, but when something is to difficult for you and you get it wrong you learn

I like mostly new maths like a new story.
Maths is like a choose your own adventure book, write the wrong answer and fatal death awaits, choose the right answer and a glorious victory to awaits, choose to do the hard page or shall I seek help from the wizard (the teacher). So maths is not all bad if look at it my way.

I like writing in my maths journal, because I can scream and shout without making a noise

2 Crafting characters

Writing is a craft, just like pottery, or designing a car or a house. When writers write, they work hard to produce novels, poems, plays and filmscripts. You are going to build up some of the craft skills of a writer as you work through the rest of the module.

You will be focusing on stories and how to construct them: you will also be talking and reading about characters, events and settings and how to use language to make these up.

Discuss

In pairs, discuss your favourite story characters; you can choose them from TV programmes and comics as well as books.

Focus on:
▶ why you like or dislike a particular character (look at what he or she does, thinks or feels)
▶ how the writer makes the character seem real and how he or she makes the character very predictable. If you are not sure about this idea, think about Tom and Jerry or any other cartoon characters who always behave in similar ways.

Presenting information

Make a class survey of favourite and least favourite characters. Use these headings:

FAVOURITE CHARACTERS   LEAST FAVOURITE CHARACTERS

When you have done the survey look at your results. Focus on these questions:
▶ Which characters are heroines?
▶ Which characters are heroes?
▶ Which characters are villains?
▶ Which characters are ordinary people?

What has your survey told you?

▶ Are heroes always huge hairy he-men?
▶ Are heroines always blonde, beautiful and helpless?
▶ Can villains be good looking?
▶ Can ordinary people be heroes, heroines or villains?

Research

Find out some names of heroes, heroines and villains in stories from other countries. Some of your classmates may be able to help. If not, try the library. Make a list of some of the reasons why they are heroes, heroines or villains. Focus on what they do, think, or feel.

To start you off, read the story on pp. 44–5.

HOW DO WRITERS MAKE UP CHARACTERS? LOOK AT KWAKU ANANSE AND A VERY GRIM TEACHER.

How Wisdom was spread throughout the World

AT ONE time, long, long ago, there was only one wise person in all the world, and that was Kwaku Ananse the spider. But, alas, Kwaku Ananse was also greedy and he wished to keep all this wisdom to himself.

One day, bored with having to stay and guard his wisdom all day, Kwaku Ananse decided to store it away and hide it in a safe place. So he called to his wife Aso and asked her to make him a big pot into which he could put all his wisdom.

Aso went down to the riverbank and collected clay. She carefully built up a great pot – a great pot with a narrow opening at the top so it could be easily sealed. Then she put the pot out in the sun to bake, and with the remainder of the clay fashioned a stopper.

When the pot was finished, Aso took it to her husband, and after making sure that there were no cracks in it, he gathered together all his wisdom and pushed it well down. He covered it with some cocoa-yam leaves, then he put in the stopper and tied it on with some strong twine.

Now Kwaku Ananse had decided to hide the pot way up in the branches of a huge silk-cotton tree that grew some distance away in the forest. It was over ten feet wide, and the spikes in its trunk would stop all but the most intrepid from climbing it.

Carrying the pot in front of him, he made his way through the forest, followed – unbeknown – by his small son Ntikuma. At last he reached the great tree and started to try climbing it. He hung the pot by a rope around his neck, with the stopper just below his nose so he could make quite sure it did not tip over.

Alas, try as he would, Kwaku Ananse could not climb the tree, for the pot got in the way of his arms and he found he was unable to grip the trunk. He tried, and he tried, and he tried. He grew hot and sticky and started to swear angrily.

Now Ntikuma was watching his father from behind a tree, puzzled by his curious antics. At last, when Kwaku Ananse's swearing grew really bad, he could stand it no longer and came up to his father timidly.

'Surely, my Father,' he said, 'if you wish to take that pot up the tree you should tie it to your back and not your front. Then your hands would be free.'

Ananse was furious. Here was his small son teaching him a lesson – a lesson which he realised was only too true. Shaking with anger and exhaustion he lifted the pot, meaning to take it off and chastise his son. His hands were slippery with sweat and the great pot was heavy. It slipped through his fingers and crashed to the ground.

The pot burst open and its contents were scattered far and wide. There was a storm coming, and the wind swept through the forest, lifting the wisdom and carrying it on its way. The rain poured down and swept the wisdom into the streams, which carried it into the sea. Thus was wisdom spread throughout the world.

Kwaku Ananse chased his small son home through the pouring rain, blaming him for so great a loss. But he was not really sorry the pot was broken, for he said, 'What is the use of so much wisdom if my own small son can judge better than I?'

Peggy Appiah

Was Kwaku Ananse a hero or a villain, or neither? Did he have a bit of both? Some villains are not all bad.

Would you like this man for your form teacher?

Thomas Gradgrind, sir, A man of realities. A man of facts and calculations. A man who proceeds upon the principle that two and two are four, and nothing over, and who is not to be talked into allowing for anything over. . . . With a rule and a pair of scales, and the multiplication table always in his pocket, sir, and always ready to weigh and measure any parcel of human nature, and tell you exactly what it comes to.

Mr Gradgrind is a character in a novel by Charles Dickens called *Hard Times*. He is a schoolteacher who believes that facts are the most important part of life. The writer is giving us a picture of Mr Gradgrind introducing himself to other people.

Here is Mr Gradgrind in the classroom. Sissy Jupe (Girl number twenty) comes from a family who work in a circus.

'Girl number twenty,' said Mr Gradgrind, squarely pointing with his square forefinger, 'I don't know that girl. Who is that girl?'
'Sissy Jupe, sir,' explained number twenty, blushing, standing up, and curtseying.
'Sissy is not a name,' said Mr Gradgrind. 'Don't call yourself Sissy. Call yourself Cecilia.'
'It's father as calls me Sissy, sir,' returned the young girl in a trembling voice.
'Then he has no business to do it,' said Mr Gradgrind. 'Tell him he mustn't. Cecilia Jupe. Let me see. What is your father?'
'He belongs to the horse-riding, if you please, sir.'
Mr Gradgrind frowned.
'We don't want to know anything about that, here. You mustn't tell us about that, here. Your father breaks horses, don't he?'
'If you please, sir, when they can get any to break, they do break horses in the ring, sir.'
'You mustn't tell us about the ring, here. Very well, then. Describe your father as a horsebreaker. He doctors sick horses, I dare say?'
'Oh yes, sir.'
'Very well, then. He is a veterinary surgeon, a farrier, and horsebreaker. Give me your definition of a horse.'
(Sissy Jupe thrown into the greatest alarm by this demand.)
'Girl number twenty unable to define a horse!' said Mr Gradgrind.
'Girl number twenty possessed of no facts, in reference to one of the commonest of animals! Some boy's definition of a horse. Bitzer, yours.'
'Quadruped. Graminivorous. Forty teeth, namely twenty-four grinders, four eye-teeth, and twelve incisive. Sheds coat in the spring; in marshy countries, sheds hoofs too. Hoofs hard, but requiring to be shod with iron. Age known by marks in mouth.' Thus (and much more) Bitzer.
'Now girl number twenty,' said Mr Gradgrind, 'you know what a horse is.'

From *Hard Times*, Charles Dickens

Discuss and improvise

Read the passage again. In groups, discuss what sort of a teacher Mr Gradgrind is.

What impression of Mr Gradgrind does the writer make for us? Imagine him teaching at your school. Choose any subject and improvise part of a Mr Gradgrind lesson. One person should be Mr Gradgrind: the rest should be pupils.

Guidelines for improvisation

▶ In groups, brainstorm ideas on Mr Gradgrind as a teacher.
▶ Choose the best ideas and work them into a short scene.
▶ Discuss how the scene went and try to polish it.
▶ When all groups are ready, watch each other's scenes and note down what was good, what was less good, about them.
▶ Discuss which group best illustrated the character of Mr Gradgrind as a teacher.

Discuss and write

Think about Mr Gradgrind's love of facts: in groups, discuss what kind of a character he is at home. In the novel he has a wife and daughter. Focus on these points:

▶ Mr Gradgrind's thoughts about his breakfast
▶ Mrs Gradgrind's thoughts about Mr Gradgrind
▶ Louisa Gradgrind's thoughts about her family at breakfast
▶ Mr Gradgrind's rules for family life – is he relaxed? Does he get cross when anything goes wrong?
▶ what the Gradgrind family might talk about.

In your groups, write a short dialogue, or conversation, between Mr Gradgrind and his wife or daughter. Focus on:

▶ Mr Gradgrind's love of facts
▶ his feeling that he is always right
▶ the topics the Gradgrind family are allowed to talk about.

You can set the conversation at a mealtime, or when they are in the garden, or out for a walk. Remember the importance of facts in Mr Gradgrind's life.

A really crucial guide to

Writing dialogue

There are two main ways of setting out a dialogue.

MR GRADGRIND	Define the object upon my plate, Mrs Gradgrind!
MRS GRADGRIND	My dear Mr Gradgrind, I think it was a kipper.
MR GRADGRIND	Mrs Gradgrind unable to define the object upon my plate!

This is how a script looks. You can add information to a dialogue script like this.

JOHN	(sitting at his desk, looking very miserable) Please, Miss, I can't spell hypotenuse.
TEACHER	(trying to be patient because **JOHN** always gets stuck in her lessons) Look it up in your dictionary. It begins with aitch. (Someone falls off their chair and **TEACHER** becomes very cross.)
TEACHER	This classroom is not a circus! Everyone sit down quietly!

The names of the characters are in capital letters at the left side of the page. Each time a character begins to speak, you put his/her name on a new line.

You underline all additional information about characters, and put it in brackets.

Use a separate line if you want to give other information, for example about things happening in the situation, such as the pupil falling off a chair. Again bracket and underline it.

You can also set out dialogue like this.

'Nice day today, Mrs Pugh,' said Mr Pugh, glaring ferociously at his wife. 'I didn't catch that,' replied Mrs Pugh, her eyes engrossed in the financial page of the paper. 'But you'll catch this in a minute,' muttered Mr Pugh, reaching for the carving knife.

This layout is used in stories. Check the stories you are reading this term for the way they set out dialogue.

You have to use quotation marks ' ' to show the actual words of a speaker. They are boundary markers. Inside the quotation marks you write the speaker's words. Begin each speech with a capital letter. Outside the quotation marks you write the linking words, such as *said Mr Pugh*.

You can give the reader more information, by adding on a commentary about the speaker's actions, thoughts and feelings.

For example:
Mr Pugh, *who was feeling very happy because he had just won the pools*, said 'I wonder if we can buy that new car tomorrow.'

The words in italic tell the reader more about Mr Pugh's feelings, and help to make his speech more easily understood.

When you write stories, you can make your characters speak as part of the story's events and actions. Look back at the way Dickens uses dialogue to set up part of his story about Mr Gradgrind and Sissy Jupe in the classroom (p. 46).

3 Bringing them to life

Point of view

Writers have to make their characters seem real by making them do things, have thoughts and feelings. When you write about characters, so do you. As you make up a character you choose your words carefully to show what sort of a person or animal it is. You are beginning to express a point of view, that is, how you see the character and how you want the reader to see him or her. Ian's story in Module 1: Speaking and Listening showed you how he saw the accident – he made a point of view for his listeners.

Look at this example:

The cat walked through the garden.

If you wanted to make the cat more interesting to your reader you could change the word 'walked' to another verb which showed your point of view on the cat more clearly.

For instance you could write
'prowled' 'crept' 'slunk' 'wandered' 'raced' 'miaoued' 'ambled' 'padded'.

If you chose 'prowled' or 'crept', how were you imagining the cat? If you chose 'ambled' or 'padded', was the cat different?

Writing

Try writing a list of verbs you could use for some other animals' movement such as snakes, spiders, elephants, camels, rats, bees, birds. Make as many different points of view as you can for each animal.

Compare your lists with a partner's. Try to agree on the points of view which each word gives the reader.

When you write you can make your point of view visible to your reader. Look at these examples.

1a I jumped up at 7 a.m. and made mum a drink, then I fed the cat and tidied up my bedroom.
1b Mum threw me out of bed at 7 a.m., forced a drink down me, fed the cat and made me tidy my bedroom.

What points of view are expressed in 1a and 1b?

2a When dad came home I was really fed up. I shouted at him for not buying me the tape I wanted and went to my room. I hated everybody.
2b When dad came home I was really pleased. I hugged him although he couldn't buy me the tape I wanted and made him a cup of tea. I felt great.

How are different points of view signalled in 2a and 2b?

WRITERS ALWAYS HAVE AN ANGLE ON WHAT THEY WRITE. FIND OUT HOW IT HAPPENS.

Writing

Here is a version of the story of St George and the Dragon.

Once upon a time, in a really wild part of England, there was a young Christian knight called George. He was amazingly brave and handsome, and not afraid of anything. One day he was riding past Lake Dreadful, where a terrible, evil fire-breathing dragon lived. This disgusting dragon had trapped the king's daughter and had just got her ready to put her in his cooking pot. She was crying bitter tears: 'O for a handsome man to save me!' came from her lips. She was blonde and beautiful and completely helpless, so George felt all his manly character stirred by her plight. He thundered in on his charger and rescued the helpless girl, having first disposed of the dragon with a single blow. The king and his people were so pleased they all became Christians and George the knight became St George.

With your partner, discuss the writer's point of view on the characters and the story. Focus on the key words the writer uses to create a point of view; for example, why is the dragon 'terrible' and 'evil'?

Then try to produce a version of the story from either the dragon's or the girl's point of view. Focus on the way the dragon or the girl could see the situation. You could make it funny by choosing your words carefully.

A really crucial guide to..

**Grumpy old woman –
might be easy
pickings**

**Get Red Riding Hood
to come close,
then snap!**

Boring old forest

**Help, that axe
looks sharp**

**Disguise myself
as grumpy
grandma**

**Go for it,
Wolfie**

**Easy to dispose
of the old woman –
throw her in the cellar**

**Worth the risk
for something to eat?**

**Nasty prissy little
girl (Red Riding Hood)**

**Even nastier
mad axeman
(the woodcutter)**

Drafting and editing

1 Write down all your ideas as quickly as you can. This is called **brainstorming** – the first stage of the writing process.

2 Make a **web diagram** of your ideas as you develop them. Here is an example for *Little Red Riding Hood* told from the wolf's point of view.

3 Try to put your ideas in order. Use those from your diagram and list them in the order you think you will write about them. You can change the order later if you want.

4 Write the first draft of your version of the St George story. Do not worry about spelling and punctuation at this stage.

5 Revise your first draft. Look at it closely to see if there are any parts you can improve; you might want to change some words, or add some, or even delete some. Then swap with the pair next to you and see what they think you might do to improve it.

6 Editing. You have now written down all you wish to say and in the way you think it is best to say it. Check the spelling, the punctuation and the sentence structure.

7 Spelling. You need a dictionary to check words you cannot spell. (Do not forget that a dictionary begins with 'a' and ends with 'z'. Where would you expect to find 'aardvark', 'necessary' or 'xylophone'? Look at the guidelines for spelling on this page for more help.)

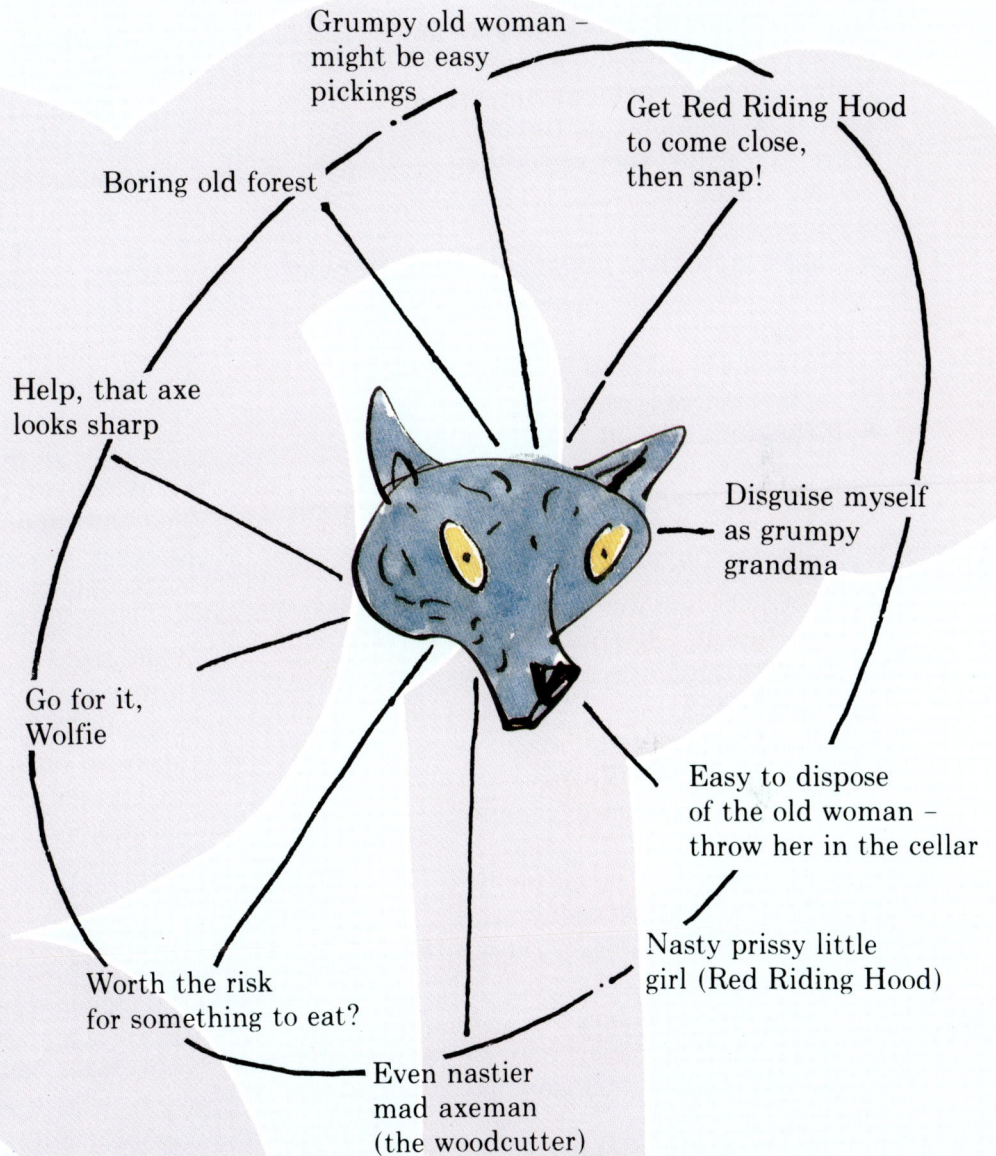

8 Look at how you are using capital letters and full stops. This will help you to make the beginnings and endings of your sentences clear to your reader. (You will find more help with punctuation on p. 52.)

A really crucial guide to....

Spelling 1

1 Write two or three spellings of the word you are not sure about. If one looks right. . .

2 Check it in a dictionary. If you cannot find it, check with a partner to see if he or she knows. Finally, check with your teacher.

3 When you have found the correct spelling of the word you want write it into your log, in the spelling pages.

4 Use your eyes! Words are all around us – in the streets, in shops, in newspapers and comics, in books, in forms to fill in, in school. Make sure you know how to spell the names of your other subjects, like mathematics, geography, science, history, home economics and any others you do.

5 Do not be frightened to try new words when you write; you can always check their spelling at the editing stage.

6 Some rules:

▶ To get more than one of something you add an *s*
one cat, two cats
but if the word ends in s, add *es*
one loss, two losses.

▶ If the word ends in x and z, add *es*
one cox, two coxes
but some words ending in x follow different rules
one ox, two oxen.

▶ When you find words which end in o they usually add *s*. Keep a record in your spelling pages of those which do not, like hero – these add *es*, heroes.

▶ You add *ed* or *ing* to process words, or verbs, when you need to change their function (what they do in a sentence or phrase)
I kick the ball
I kicked the ball last night
I am kicking the ball now.
Some words, like bake, cut out the first e, and add *ed* or *ing*
bake baked baking.
Keep a note of these when you need to. Some, like rap, double their final letter and then add *ed* or *ing*
rap rapped rapping.
There are more spelling rules and guidelines in Module 6: Writing.

A really crucial guide to

Punctuation 1

When you write, you need to make your writing clear to your readers. They need to know how many words to read as a section of a sentence, and when your sentences begin and end.

In your final editing you should aim to use capital letters, full stops and commas accurately. When do you use them?

1 **Capital letters**
a) for the first letter of people's names:
Bill Bones, Hetty Harbottle, Fred Smith
of places:
Paris, Tokyo, Moscow, London
of weekdays:
Friday, Saturday, Sunday
of months:
August, September, October
of TV programme titles:
Eastenders, Home and Away, Blue Peter
of book titles:
Crummy Mummy and Me
b) for the first letter of a sentence:
He swam the Channel.
She flew to Australia.
c) When you use 'I':
As I thought, there's no sugar left.
d) when you are writing down speech, at the beginning of a fresh piece of speech:
She said, 'Don't ask me again, please.'
What other examples can you find?

2 **Full stops**
Many sentences which you write end with fullstops. (Just like the one you have read.)
He forgot the bacon.
Catch me a fat trout.

3 **Commas**
Writers use commas to break up sentences. Between your opening capital letter, which signals the start of a new sentence, and the full stop, which signals the end of the sentence, writers sometimes need to use a large number of words. Look at the last sentence: there are 34 words in it. It is broken up into sections by commas, so that the reader doesn't get lost trying to read it all at once.
Commas can:
a) mark off each item in a list
Four candles, fork handles, five night lights, six mousetraps, please.
He ate seven sausages, eight octopuses, nine nectarines, and then felt sick.
b) show the clause boundaries in a sentence
When the cat had finished her dinner, she licked her lips.
Although it was snowing hard, his face was glowing with heat

There are more punctuation guidelines on p. 131.

4 Naming the names and ringing the changes

Writers give their characters names which often suggest what kinds of people the characters are.

Discuss and write

What sorts of characters do these character names suggest? In pairs, write a mini-saga about one of them. A mini-saga is a story which you have to write in exactly 50 words. Try it!

Character Names: Mr Krook
Mr Bumble
Mrs Jellyby
Bronco Bullfrog
Nasty Roche
Psychogran

Giving a character a name can help you to suggest a point of view about that character. What else must the writer think about when she or he is writing?

Some of his or her thoughts must go on what the characters do, think and feel.

Discuss and write

With a partner, read the passages below and discuss the way the writer makes each character think, feel and act.

Cinderella had never been so happy in all her life. Her little feet twinkling in their crystal slippers kept perfect step with the prince, and they both began to wish, more than anything else, that they could be together always. Then the clock struck a quarter to twelve, and Cinderella had to tear herself away from the prince and run out to her waiting pumpkin coach.

From *The Sleeping Beauty and other tales*, C. Perrault

Once there was a great Prince who was so great a fighter that no one dared to deny him anything that he asked, and people would give up their houses and lands, their children, and even their own freedom rather than offend him.

Everything the people had was his at the asking, they feared him so, and would tremble and shake when he came thundering past on his war horse, whose breath was fire. And they feared his sword, which was so sharp that it wounded the wind as it cut through it, and his battle-axe that could cut the world in half – or so they said – and his frown that was like a cloud, and his voice that was like thunder – or so they said.

From *The Prince and the Goose Girl*, Elinor Mordant

With your partner, make some changes to each passage to alter the writer's point of view on each character.

HAVE A GO AT MAKING SOME CHARACTERS FROM YOUR OWN WORDS.

Compare your results with other pairs/groups in the class. Focus on:
▶ which words you changed
▶ why you changed them
▶ the difference the changes made.

Writers make up characters who have names, who think, feel and act. If they do not like the results they can change them by choosing different words. This is part of the writer's power over language. It has its limits, however. Once you have started writing a horror story, it might not be sensible to put in a passage about little children playing happily in a school playground – or could it be sensible?

Discuss

With a partner, discuss some unlikely combinations of characters from different types of story. How many can you make?

Here is an example: Mickey Mouse and Frankenstein

When writers write stories they know that there are patterns which their readers expect them to follow. For Mickey Mouse to meet Frankenstein the writer has broken the expected patterns. Who does Mickey Mouse normally meet?

Write

Try writing some invitations to dinner from one of your character pairs. Keep your choice of words suitable for the character.

Here is an example:

Your lists of character combinations should lead you to the next stage of your thinking about writing stories: the setting, or where action happens.

INVITATION
DENNIS the MENACE
TO SOFTY WALTER.
GRUB AND MENACING FUN
AT SIX O'CLOCK. HAR HAR

5 Scene setting

Discuss and write

With a partner, discuss the settings of your favourite TV shows, comics and advertisements.

Make a ten question quiz for other pairs in your class about the settings, such as:

> Which town does Desperate Dan live in?

Try the quiz out with other pairs in your class, then, in groups, discuss which characters you could put in the area where you live, and why.

Now, read the following passage and, with a partner, brainstorm some ideas for what might happen in this setting. Discuss what you think the

writer is trying to make the reader feel about the place. Try to identify which words and phrases show the atmosphere most clearly.

It was already day, a windless and sullen morning, and the marsh-reeks lay in heavy banks. No sun pierced the low clouded sky. After a brief rest they set out again and were soon lost in a shadowy silent world, cut off from all view of the lands about.

It was dreary and wearisome. Cold clammy winter still held sway in this forsaken country. The only green was the scum of livid weed on the dark greasy surfaces of the sullen waters. Dead grasses and rotting reeds loomed up in the mists like ragged shadows of long-forgotten summers.

Write

With your partner, try writing settings for some of these characters:

▶ a lonely tramp
▶ a football-crazy boy or girl
▶ a prisoner on the run
▶ a mad scientist
▶ a snake charmer.

Now think about what these characters might be doing. What could the mad scientist be up to, for instance? When you write stories you have to invent the actions or events which your characters get involved in, and where these all happen.

So, you need to focus on **events** and **actions**.

Discuss and write

A story for 7–8-year-old children is printed on p. 56. The printer has muddled the order of actions and events. Using the pictures (below and on p. 56), work out the order of actions and events which you think is right for the story. Make notes about your reasons as you discuss what to do.

Then write a mini-saga about one of the giants for a class of 7–8-year-olds. Keep your story to 50 words exactly. If you can, read your mini-sagas to some children in the local primary school and ask them what they think of them.

EXPLORE SOME NASTY SETTINGS, AND THINK OF SOME CHARACTERS TO GO WITH THEM. WRITE A MINI SAGA FOR SOME PRIMARY CHILDREN.

1 The two giants were so sad they could not think what to do. They sat down and cried so much, they made a great storm of giant tears.

2 But she did not see the hammer. It landed on the top of her head and she fell down and died.

3 The giant who lives on St Michael's Mount and the giant who lived on Trecrobben Hill were shoemakers. But they only had one hammer.

4 Some people say they lifted up the church and buried the giant's wife under it. Others say they just rolled her down the hill into the sea.

5 Giant Trecrobben picked it up and threw it over the water. 'Look out!' he shouted, 'here it comes.'

6 One day the giant on St Michael's Mount shouted to his friend, 'Hello, giant Trecrobben. Please will you lend me the hammer?'

7 The wife of the giant on St Michael's Mount was in her cave. She ran out when she heard the shouting.

6 Variations on a theme

Read the stories 'Frederick and Catherine' and 'Gone is Gone'. Discuss with your partner how each story works. Focus on:
▶ How are the characters built up? Look at their thoughts, feelings and actions.
▶ Do the characters fit the settings and

situations? If not, why not?
▶ Which events and actions are important for the way the story moves from beginning to end?
▶ How does the writer make his or her point of view in each story and what is it?
▶ Which point of view do you prefer?

FREDERICK AND CATHERINE

THERE was once a man called Frederick: he had a wife whose name was Catherine, and they had not long been married. One day Frederick said, 'Kate! I am going to work in the fields; when I come back I shall be hungry, so let me have something nice cooked, and a good draught of ale.' 'Very well,' said she, 'it shall all be ready.' When dinnertime drew nigh, Catherine took a nice steak and put it on the fire to fry. The steak soon began to look brown, and to crackle in the pan; and Catherine stood by with a fork and turned it: then she said to herself, 'The steak is almost ready, I may as well go to the cellar for the ale.' So she left the pan on the fire, and took a large jug and went into the cellar and tapped the ale cask. The beer ran into the jug, and Catherine stood looking on. At last it popped into her head, 'The dog is not shut up – he may be running away with the steak; that's well thought of.' So up she ran from the cellar; and sure enough the rascally cur had got the steak in his mouth, and was making off with it.

Away ran Catherine, and away ran the dog across the field! but he ran faster than she, and stuck close to the steak. 'It's all gone, and "what can't be cured must be endured,"' said Catherine.

Now all this time the ale was running too, for Catherine had not turned the cock; and when the jug was full the liquor ran upon the floor till the cask was empty. When she got to the cellar stairs she saw what had happened. 'My stars!' said she, 'what shall I do to keep Frederick from seeing all this slopping about?' So she thought a while; and at last remembered that there was a sack of fine meal bought at the last fair, and that if she sprinkled this over the floor it would suck up the ale nicely. So away she went for it: but she managed to set it down

just upon the great jug full of beer, and upset it; and thus all the ale that had been saved was set swimming on the floor also. 'Ah! well,' said she, 'when one goes, another may as well follow.'

At noon Frederick came home. 'Now, wife,' cried he, 'what have you for dinner?' 'O Frederick!' answered she, 'I was cooking you a steak; but while I went down to draw the ale, the dog ran away with it; and while I ran after him, the ale all ran out; and when I went to dry up the ale with the sack of meal that we got at the fair, I upset the jug: but the cellar is now quite dry, and looks so clean!' 'Kate, Kate,' said he, 'how could you do all this? Why did you leave the steak to fry, and the ale to run, and then spoil all the meal?' 'Why, Frederick,' said she, 'I did not know I was doing wrong, you should have told me before.'

The husband had a good deal of gold in the house: so he said to Catherine, 'What pretty yellow buttons these are! I shall put them into a box and bury them in the garden; but take care that you never go near or meddle with them.' 'No, Frederick,' said she, 'that I never will.' As soon as he was gone, there came by some pedlars with earthenware plates and dishes, and they asked her whether she would buy. 'Oh dear me, I should like to buy very much, but I have no money: if you had any use for yellow buttons, I might deal with you.' 'Yellow buttons!' said they: 'let us have a look at them.' 'Go into the garden and dig where I tell you, and you will find the yellow buttons: I dare not go myself.' So the rogues went: and when they found what these yellow buttons were, they took them all away, and left her plenty of plates and dishes. Then she set them all about the house for a show: and when Frederick came back, he cried out, 'Kate, what have you been doing?' 'See,' said she, 'I have bought all these with your yellow buttons: but I did not touch them myself; the pedlars went themselves and dug them up.' 'Wife, wife,' said Frederick, 'those yellow buttons were all my money: How came you to do such a thing?' 'Why,' answered she, 'I did not know there was any harm in it; you should have told me.'

Catherine stood musing for a while, and at last said to her husband, 'Frederick, we will soon get the gold back: let us run after the thieves.' 'Well, we will try,' answered he; 'but take some butter and cheese with you, that we may have something to eat by the way.' 'Very well,' said she; and they set out: and as Frederick walked the fastest, he left his wife some way behind. 'It does not matter,' thought she: 'when we turn back, I shall be so much nearer home than he.'

Presently she came to the top of a hill; down the side of which were was a road so narrow that the cart-wheels always chafed the trees on each side as they passed. 'Ah, see now,' said she, 'how they have bruised and wounded those poor trees; they will never get well.' So she took pity on them, and made use of the butter to grease them all, so that the wheels might not hurt them so much. While she was doing this kind office, one of her cheeses fell out of the basket, and rolled down the hill. Catherine looked, but could not see where it was gone; so she said, 'Well, I suppose the other will go the same way and find you; he has younger legs than I have.' Then she rolled the other cheese after it; and away it went, nobody knows where, down the hill.

At last she overtook Frederick, who desired her to give him something to eat. Then she gave him the dry bread. 'Where are the butter and cheese?' said he. 'Oh!' answered she, 'I used the butter to grease those poor trees that the wheels chafed so: and one of the cheeses ran away, so I sent the other after it to find it, and I suppose they are both on the road together somewhere.' 'What a goose you are to do such silly things!' said the husband. 'How can you say so?' said she; 'I am sure you never told me not.'

They ate the dry bread together; and Frederick said, 'Kate, I hope you locked the door safe when you came away.' 'No,' answered she, 'you did not tell me.' 'Then go home, and do it now before we go any farther,' said Frederick, 'and bring with you something to eat.'

Catherine did as he told her, and thought to herself by the way, 'Frederick wants something to eat; but I don't think he is very fond of butter and cheese: I'll bring him a bag of fine nuts, and the vinegar, for I have often seen him take some.'

When she reached home, she bolted the back door, but the front door she took off the hinges, and said, 'Frederick told me to lock the door, but surely it can no where be so safe as if I take it with me.' So she took her time by the way: and when she overtook her husband she cried out, 'There, Frederick, there is the door itself, now you may watch it as carefully as you please.' 'Alas! alas!' said he, 'what a clever wife I have! I sent you to make the house fast, and you take the door away, so that every body may go in and out as they please: – however, as you have brought the door, you shall carry it about with you for your pains.' 'Very well,' answered she, 'I'll carry the door; but I'll not carry the nuts and vinegar bottle also, – that would be too much of a load; so, if you please, I'll fasten them to the door.'

They set off into the wood to look for the thieves; but they could not find them: and when it grew dark, they climbed up into a tree to spend the night there. Scarcely were they up, than who should come by but the very rogues they were looking for. They sat down and made a fire under the very tree where Frederick and Catherine were. Frederick slipped down on the other side, and picked up some stones. Then he climbed up again, and tried to hit the thieves on the head with them: but they only said, 'It must be near morning, for the wind shakes the fir-apples down.'

Catherine, who had the door on her shoulder, began to be very tired; but she thought it was the nuts upon it that were so heavy: so she said softly, 'Frederick, I must let the nuts go.' 'No,' answered he, 'not now, they will discover us.' 'I can't help that, they must go.' 'Well then, make haste and throw them down, if you will.' Then away rattled the nuts down among the boughs; and one of the thieves cried. 'Bless me, it is hailing.'

A little while after, Catherine thought the door was still very heavy: so she whispered to Frederick, 'I must throw the vinegar down.' 'Pray don't,' answered he, 'it will discover us.' 'I can't help that,' said she, 'go it must.' So she poured all the vinegar down; and the thieves said, 'What a heavy dew there is!'

At last it popped into Catherine's head that it was the door itself that was so heavy all the time: so she whispered Frederick. 'I must throw the door down soon.' But he begged and prayed her not to do so, for he was sure it would betray them. 'Here goes, however,' said she: and down went the door with such a clatter upon the thieves, that they cried out 'Murder!' and not knowing what was coming, ran away as fast as they could, and left all the gold. So when Frederick and Catherine came down, there they found all their money safe and sound.

GONE IS GONE

In the north country, where grass grows on the roofs of the cottages, there once lived a farmer who was not pleased with his lot in life. 'I do more work in a day than you do in three,' he said to his wife almost every noon-time and evening when he came in from the fields. 'I toil and sweat, ploughing and sowing and harvesting, while you laze around the house.'

At last his wife grew tired of hearing this talk. 'Very well, husband,' she said. 'Tomorrow I will do your work, and you can do mine. I'll go out to cut the hay, and you can stay here and keep the house.' 'Good,' the husband said, and he laughed to himself, thinking how easy it would be.

So the next morning the wife put the scythe over her shoulder and went out into the fields. Her husband thought he would begin by churning the cream, so there would be butter for the porridge at dinner. He churned and he churned, yet the butter did not come. 'This is hot work,' he said, and he went out the cottage door and down into the cellar to get some ale.

But just as he turned the tap on the barrel, he heard a noise overhead, which was the pig coming into the cottage, because he had left the door open. He ran up the cellar steps as fast as he could, but he was too late. The pig had already knocked over the churn, and was rooting and grunting in it. The husband shouted and ran at the pig, and booted him out the door. Then he turned and looked at the churn lying on its side with the cream spilt over the floor.

'Well,' he said. 'Gone is gone.'

Then he remembered the ale, and ran back down the cellar. But he had left the tap open, and all the ale had run out of the barrel, so that there was none left to drink.

'Well, gone is gone,' he said again.

Now the husband thought he would grind some oatmeal for the porridge. But while he was doing this he heard the cow mooing in the barn, and remembered that she was still shut up in her stall and had had nothing to eat all morning. As he hurried to let her out, he saw that the sun was already high in the sky. He thought that it was too late and too far to lead the cow down the meadow, and that instead he would cut her some grass from

the cottage roof, for a fine crop was growing there.

Then he said to himself that it would be much easier if he could only get the cow herself onto the roof. So he laid a plank across from the hill at the back of the cottage, and fetched her out of her stall. She didn't want to go onto the roof very much; but he pulled and coaxed and at last he got her over. Then he thought he had better tie her up, so she wouldn't fall off. So he fastened a rope to her halter, and out the other end down the chimney.

He climbed down off the roof and hurried back into the cottage. It was full of chickens, for he had left the door open again, and they had got into the oats. He shouted and ran at the chickens and shooed them out the door. Then he turned and looked at the bowl knocked over, and all the oatmeal that he had ground scattered over the floor.

'Well,' he said. 'Gone is gone.'

He took the end of the cow's rope that was hanging down the chimney and tied it around his leg. Then he filled the big iron kettle with water and hung it over the fire, for it was dinner-time; and as fast as he could he ground more oats. The water began to boil, and he put them in. But while he was doing this, the cow fell off the roof, and as she fell she dragged the husband up the chimney by his leg. There he stuck fast, shouting and cursing; and as for the cow, she hung halfway down the wall outside.

It was now long past noon, and the wife, who had been cutting hay all morning, grew tired of waiting for her husband to call her home to dinner and started back to the cottage. As she came up the hill the first thing she saw was the cow hanging from the roof. She ran up and cut the rope with her scythe, and the cow fell to the ground. At the same time, inside, down fell her husband headfirst into the kettle of porridge.

The wife heard the noise and ran into the cottage. There was spilt cream and oats everywhere, and a smell of ale from the cellar, and her husband upside down in the kettle. She pulled him out, and there he stood on the floor dripping porridge.

'Well, husband,' said she, 'Gone is gone. From today forth, you do your work, and I'll do mine, and we'll say no more about it.'

You have been reflecting, or looking closely and thinking about some things which writers do to make stories.

Some stories begin with 'Once upon a time . . .' and you know they will go on with . . . with what? How could you continue a story which began that way? In pairs, brainstorm some ideas for two possible stories.

Other stories begin in very different ways. Read the beginnings of these stories and try to predict what the rest of the story might be. You could write web diagrams for the two you like best.

1 I went down on my knees upon the brand-new linoleum, and smelled the strange smell. It was rich and oily. It first entered and attached itself to something in my memory when I was nine years old. I've since learned that it is the smell of linseed oil, but coming on it unexpectedly can make me both a little disturbed and sad.

Edna O'Brien

2 George Adams finished his coffee, mashed out his cigarette in the saucer, and stood up.

'I'm off,' he said to his wife as he went to the coat closet. 'See you around six.'

'Don't forget Bobby's school,' she said.

Adams stopped, and looked at her. 'What about it?' he asked.

'They're having Fathers' Day,' she said. 'Remember?'

'Oh, my God,' Adams said. He paused, then said hurriedly, 'I can't make it. It's out of the question.'

'You've got to,' she said. 'You missed it last year, and he was terribly hurt. Just go for a few minutes, but you've *got* to do it. I promised him I'd remind you.'

Adams drew a deep breath and said nothing.

'Bobby said you could just come for the English class,' Eleanor went on. 'Between twelve twenty and one. Please don't let him down again.'

'Well, I'll try,' Adams said. 'I'll make it if I can.'

Nathaniel Benchley

3 The sun had just started coming up when the men gathered at the gate of the White Plantation. They leaned on the fence, waiting. No one was nervous, though. They'd all been waiting a long time. A few more minutes couldn't make much difference. They surveyed the land that they were leaving, the land from which they had brought forth seas of cotton.

Jean Wheeler Smith

4 'Hit him again,' said my father, so I hit the stranger in the face and stood over him as he fell heavily into the grass, powdery with small white seeds. He made no attempt to get up, but lay on his back, staring into our faces and licking his lips. A few seeds clung to his hair and stuck in the trickle of blood that oozed from one nostril.

'Get up,' said my father, but the stranger shook his head.

'Stay there, then,' said my father and, taking out his tobacco-pouch, he rolled a cigarette while he made up his mind what to do next.

Philip Oakes

5 Unlike the Centre Court at Wimbledon, the Centre Court at our school is the one nobody wants to play on. It is made of asphalt and has dents in it, like Ryvita. All the other courts are grass, out in the sun: Centre Court is between the science block and the canteen and when there is a Governors' Meeting the governors use it as a car park. The sun only shines on Centre Court at noon in June and there is green algae growing round the edges. When I volunteered to be an umpire at the annual tennis tournament I might have known that I was going to end up on Centre Court.

Jan Mark

6 She walked through flowers, the girl, ox-eye daisies and vetch and cow parsley, keeping to the track at the edge of the field. She could see the cottage in the distance, shrugged down into the dip beyond the next hedge. 'Mrs Rutter,' Pat had said, 'Mrs Rutter at Nether Cottage, you don't know her, Sandra? She's a dear old thing, all on her own, of course, we try to keep an eye. A wonky leg after her op. and the home help's off with a bad back this week. So could you make that your Saturday afternoon session, dear? Lovely. There'll be one of the others, I'm not sure who.'

Penelope Lively

7 'Are you ever coming?' asked the boy.

'Soon,' she said. She knew he would not go fishing without her. He had bought bait, made sandwiches, filled a bottle with lemonade, sorted his tackle – everything was put ready by the open door. He was waiting outside the door in the sunlight.

'Come on, it's late.'

'It's not.'

'What are you doing?'

She was at the mirror by the sink fixing her hair into a pony tail with a new tortoiseshell clip. Trying to.

'I'll go alone.'

She just knew he wouldn't;

Hilary Tunnicliffe

8 I wanted a bike more than anything else in the world. I kept dropping hints. It wasn't difficult for them to know what I wanted. It was my birthday two weeks ago. I couldn't get to sleep the night before, I was so excited. I had hinted and hinted, and I was sure this time I would get one. When I'd asked before, they'd pulled faces, but they *had* said, perhaps, when I was older. Well, I was older now, wasn't I? Surely fourteen was old enough.

Susan Gregory

9 He lived in one of the large houses on the other side of the park. He wore grey flannel shorts, and always had a tie on. The gang did not like to judge by appearances, knowing only too well that clothes are imposed by parents, and several times, in one devious way or another, they had invited him to join them. He said his name was Lance. They did not know it was posh, and it woke an echo in their warlike minds, and so did not disgrace him.

Jill Paton Walsh

10 A man don't know what he'll do, a man don't know what he is till he gets his back pressed up against a wall. Now you take Aaron Lott: there ain't no other way to explain the crazy thing he did. He was going along fine, preaching the gospel, saving souls, and getting along with the white folks; and then, all of a sudden, he felt wood pressing against his back.

Lerone Bennett Jnr

You have read the beginnings of several stories, each of which is different from the 'Once upon a time' you can find in fairy stories or folk tales. The 'Once upon a time' beginning makes the reader expect a certain kind of story, with a pattern of characters, settings and situations, and events and actions all fitting into his or her expectations.

But hold on – what is a beginning? Does it have to be 'Once upon a time'?

If you look back at a well known story like 'Little Red Riding Hood' you can plot the story events in several different ways.

Little Red Riding Hood's story

TIME LINE

1   2   3   4   5

Version 1
Little Red Riding Hood takes some cakes through the forest to her grandma.

She meets the big bad wolf and tells him what she's doing and where she's going.

The wolf hurries on ahead and bundles Grandma into the cellar.

Red Riding Hood enters the house and mistakes the wolf for her grandmother.

The wolf tries to eat Red Riding Hood but the woodcutter comes and kills him.

Version 2
Wolf thinks, 'What shall I do today? I'm hungry.'

Meets Red Riding Hood and plots to eat her at her Grandma's house.

Wolf rushes on to Grandma's, seizes her and puts her in the cellar.

Wolf puts on Grandma's clothes and waits for Red Riding Hood.

Wolf tries to fool Red Riding Hood but the woodcutter arrives – he escapes, just.

Version 3
Woodcutter is in the pub. He tells the story about the wolf and Red Riding Hood. He begins with, 'Do you know what happened yesterday?'

Tells his mates about the screams coming from Grandma's cottage.

Finds Red Riding Hood about to be eaten by the wolf.

He chases the wolf and kills it with one blow of the axe.

Asks Red Riding Hood what has happened and finds out her story.

Version 4
Red Riding Hood is bored by the summer holidays. She asks her mother for something to do. She is given cakes to take through the forest to Grandma.

Meets the wolf and thinks 'What a nasty character he is – I'll bet he tries to get me. I must make a plan.'

Meets woodcutter, and tells him to be at Grandma's, listening for her cries of 'Help, help!'

Goes to Grandma's, meets wolf, plays wolf's game to fool him for a while.

Screams to woodcutter who comes and kills wolf.

7 The story kit game

For two players

You need: a dice, a pen or pencil, a note book.

Rules

1 Each player throws the dice. The one with the higher score starts the game.
2 The players throw the dice in turn until one gets an *even* number. Then a **character** is chosen from the list.
3 Both players brainstorm some ideas about the character, and keep notes.
4 The players continue to throw the dice in turn until the other player gets an even number and can choose a character. Then repeat rule 3.
5 Continue with rules 2–4 until each player has won at least three characters.
6 The players now throw the dice in turn until one gets an *odd* number. Then a **setting** or **location** is chosen. (The last player to win a character should let the other player start.)
7 Both players brainstorm some ideas about the setting, and keep notes.
8 Continue until each player has two settings.
9 Each player now throws the dice in turn until *any number larger than four* appears. An **action** or **event** is then chosen.
10 Both players brainstorm some ideas about the action, and keep notes.
11 Continue until each player has three actions or events.

Characters

Lazy farmworker
Energetic footballer
Crazy doctor
Pilot
Homeless teenager
Deep-sea diver
Customs officer
'Whizz-kid' business person
11–13-year-old
Teacher
Camel driver
Window cleaner
Police officer
Smuggler

Settings

Airport
City centre at night
A North Sea oil rig
A tumbledown farm
A football ground
A café
A beach
A TV studio
School
A lonely strange-looking house
Docks
Desert
A mountain
A motorway
An island

Actions or Events

Outbreak of a strange disease
A series of crimes in a shopping centre
A disaster in a lonely part of the country
A school cut off by bad weather
The theft of paper, pens and pencils
A vanishing oasis
Glass suddenly becoming very brittle
An unknown team makes headlines
A rabid animal is smuggled into Britain
A brilliant new computer is invented
An air crash or hijack
Strange visitors arrive from another planet
Unknown large plants start to grow very quickly
A plague of large birds arrive
Smugglers caught by young girls or boys

Add to these lists if you can think of any others.

Combine the characters, settings and events in any way you wish.

Write and discuss

You now have a basic story kit. Make a web diagram of your own ideas, then the first draft of your story.

Discuss with a partner the first draft, and see if you can improve each other's ideas.

Make the final edit; check spelling, punctuation, and sentence structure. Decide whether you will present the story in your best handwriting, or wordprocessing, if this is possible.

As a class decide with your teacher how best to display your stories.

1 Greetings!

I wonder how many people speak to you during the course of a day. Look back at p. 1. Here are just some of the types of people you might have referred to. Add to the list if you can:

Introduction

In Module 1 you concentrated on the times and occasions when *you* speak. In this module you will be exploring the times and occasions when people speak to you.

Sometimes it is easy to get on with other people; sometimes it is much more difficult. Sometimes there are conflicts between people when they speak to each other. Sometimes there are special situations for speaking and listening when it is important to understand how to speak or listen, as with parents and very young children.

Read on, and explore the situations in Module 4.

You will notice that each person above has an empty speech bubble. When we see people for the first time, they normally utter a few words of greeting, for example, good morning, hello, etc. Think about the people you normally speak to in the course of a day and fill in the speech bubbles for them with the words or phrases that they use to greet you.

DON'T TALK TO ME LIKE THAT! LIKE WHAT? FIND OUT WHAT AFFECTS THE LANGUAGE YOU SPEAK!

How many different types of greeting can you think of?

Let us look at these greetings a little further and find out at least one reason why we use different types of greeting.

Improvise

With a partner, use each of these greetings as starting points for an improvisation:

Improvisation 1: 'Hiya.'
'Alright?'

Improvisation 2: 'Good morning, sir.'
'Good morning.'

Improvisation 3: 'How are you?'
'Fine. How are you?'

Tell another pair what your scenes involved and then discuss these questions:
▶ Did you find when you improvised these scenes that these different greetings gave you a clue to how these people got on with one another?
▶ Which scene involved good friends?
▶ Which scene involved strangers or people who are not particularly friendly?
▶ What sorts of greeting do you use? When do you use each one?

Now let us look at the different words and phrases we use to bring meetings to an end.

In your group, brainstorm and produce a list of parting phrases or words, for example:

'Good-bye, then. Nice to meet you.'

Now, in your pairs, make up some short scenes to show who might use these parting phrases and where and how they might be used.

When you have finished, copy out the situation scale on the right and place each greeting on the scale.

to members of the family

to close friends

to people of your own age you do not know well, or do not know at all

to relations or neighbours

to adults you know only in formal situations: e.g. school, church

to adults you do not know well, or do not know at all

2 Parents and children

We found in the last unit that people tend to change the way they speak according to how they see you. We can take this a little further. Look at the transcript on p. 66 of a mother talking to her 2-year-old daughter in the kitchen. The mother is at the breakfast table and her daughter is trying to dress herself.

MOTHER What's the matter? What're you trying to do?
CHILD   I want that. (<u>pointing to sweater on a chair</u>)
MOTHER What? What do you want, sweetheart?
CHILD   I want that. I want to wear that. I weared it. . . I weared
        it to nanna's. Mummy! I want to wear that.
MOTHER Here you are then sweetheart. (<u>hands sweater to her</u>)
        Can you put it on by yourself? (<u>lifts daughter onto her</u>
        <u>lap</u>)
CHILD   Daddy coming home now.
MOTHER Yes.
CHILD   'tend daddy.
MOTHER Pretend daddy? Okay. Hello daddy, how are you?
CHILD   It's not comed yet.
MOTHER When's he coming?
CHILD   He coming from work.
MOTHER Has pretend daddy brought you some sweeties?
CHILD   No.
MOTHER What's he brought you then?
CHILD   What's them funny baby things called? (<u>pointing to</u>
        <u>mother's cereal bowl</u>)
MOTHER Rice Crispies? Snap, crackle, pop?
CHILD   Daddy like crackle pops.
MOTHER Does he?
CHILD   Daddy like crackle pops. And Holly.

Write

Read the transcript very carefully. List any words or phrases that the mother uses when she is talking to her daughter that you would not expect her to use if she was your mother talking to you.

Are there any other things she does when she is speaking that show she is talking to a very young child?

Improvise

One of you take the role of a father or mother who has never got out of the habit of talking to your son or daughter as if he or she was a 2-year-old.

The other partner is to take the role of the son or daughter. Think about the situation you find yourself in. You have just got ready to go out to the pictures. Your friend is just about to call for you. Your mother/father stops you as you go past the kitchen door, calls you into the room and begins to comment on how nice you look. How do you think you will react?

Polish your scene and present it to another group.

A

Now lad, when you get in the box I don't want to see any square balls. Just knock it on to Mike who'll flick it on with his head to Roger who'll smack it in. If it all works to plan we'll leave the keeper stranded.

SOMETIMES IT IS NOT ONLY WHAT YOU SAY THAT IS IMPORTANT, IT IS THE WAY YOU SAY IT!

Discuss

Discuss

▶ What happens when people use the wrong sort of language for the people they're talking to?

▶ How is the language your parents use now different to what it was like when you were a 2-year-old?

The poet Michael Rosen has a particular ear for the way in which parents speak to children. Here is one of his poems in which he presents some of the typical things parents say to their sons and daughters:

Chivvy

Grown-ups say things like:
Speak up.
Don't talk with your mouth full
Don't stare
Don't point
Don't pick your nose
Sit up
Say please
Less noise
Shut the door behind you
Don't drag your feet
Haven't you got a hankie?
Take your hands out of your pockets
Pull your socks up
Stand up straight
Say thank you
Don't interrupt
No one thinks you're funny
Take your elbows off the table
Can't you make up your *own*
mind about anything?

Michael Rosen

Write

Try making your own collection of any one of the following:

▶ typical things your parents say to you
▶ typical things your brother or sister says to you
▶ typical things your teachers say to you
▶ typical things other adults say to you.

Then try making a poem out of them like Michael Rosen's.

3 Subject talk

HAVE YOU EVER FELT THAT SOME TEACHERS SPEAK A FOREIGN LANGUAGE, EVEN WHEN IT IS NOT A FRENCH LESSON? FIND OUT WHY.

It is not just parents who speak to you in special ways. Have you realised that every teacher you speak to uses a slightly different language when he or she is teaching you?

Write

Imagine you are walking along a corridor in your school. You hear snatches of the different lessons that are taking place in the classrooms off the corridor. Which subject teachers said the following?

...ook at this diagram, you ...e clearly that one slab of ... sliding underneath ... See? The sediments just ...e gradually squeezed and ...by the resulting pressure.

C
It's quite easy really. The width of the rectangle is approximately the radius of the circle and its length is almost half the circumference.

D
Cross-hatching isn't easy but it's quite an effective way of achieving half-tones. The denser the cross-hatching the darker the tone.

E
You'll need to prepare a back-up. Get a disc out of the cupboard. When you've finished, prepare me a hard copy . . .

Go back and list the clues that told you which language was used in which lesson?

What conclusions can you draw from this exercise about the language you meet in different lessons?

Research

Now ask two or three of your subject teachers other than English if you can record five minutes of their lessons.

Listen to the recordings and list any words or phrases which are special to each subject area, that is, words that you are only likely to come across in each separate subject.

LANGUAGE NOTE

Each subject has its own form of language called a *register*. Understanding the idea you are working on in lessons sometimes depends on your ability to understand and use the appropriate register. Look back at p. 37.

4 Varieties

At school you are also likely to meet teachers and pupils from different parts of the country. Some may even have been born in different parts of the English-speaking world. Have you ever listened to the way they speak? They all speak slightly differently. Not only might they say the same words as you slightly differently, they may occasionally use different words when referring to the same thing as you.

Discuss

Look at this poem which attempts to capture some of these types of differences in speech.

Read it through on your own. Then discuss how you might perform the poem aloud.

A Clean Sweep

I've 'ad lots o' jobs, – some was good, some was bad, –
But the one as I counts the most strange,
Was once when I went to a millionaire's 'ouse
To sweep out the chimneys an' range.
They wanted it doin' at night, rather late,
When the fires weren't in use, arter tea, –
So I goes ter the place, an' I strolls up the drive,
About eight o'clock it 'ud be,
When I gets ter the hentrance I sees two fat blokes
Dressed in gold, an' I 'ears one say:
"'Er Ladyship 'as bin hexpectin' Yer Grace,
Will Yer Grace kindly foller this way?"
Well I looks round ter see who 'e means by "Yer Grace,"
But there weren't no one there, 'ceptin' me, –
So I think p'r'aps "Yer Grace" is the *French* word fer "sweep"
So I follows the bloke just ter see,
Then a lady, all larfin', comes out of a room,
An' ses: – as she looks at me clothes, –
"Why really, I shouldn't 'a' knowed Yer Grace,
If it weren't fer that wart on yer nose!"
Then she opens a door, an' I sees a big room
Full o' folk all dressed in strange things, –
Some was soldiers, some nurses, some sailors, some cooks,
An' sev'ral was hangels wi' wings.
Well, then the band stopped, an' the dancers sat down,
An' a fat gent comes up on me right,
An' 'e puts sev'ral coins in me fist, as 'e ses:
"There's the ten pounds I borrowed last night."
Then a lady comes up, an' ses: "Really Yer Grace
I've larfed till me sides are quite sore," –
So I ses: "Get some Zam Buk, an' rub 'em wi' that!"

An' everyone near, give a roar,
Then one ses: "Why weren't you at the hopera last night?
'Ad yer bin playin' polo or goff?'
I ses: "No I'd bin playin at *bathin' the kids,*
'Cause the missus 'ad took a night off!"
Well then us 'ad supper, – it weren't arf a spread, –
The best feed I've 'ad in me life! –
An' everyone larfed, an' sed: "Isn't 'e fine!"
When the *blankmange* slipped orf o' me knife.
An' they didn't arf roar when I upset me glass
Down a girl who was dressed all in white, –
But it didn't show much, fer I dusted 'er frock
Wi' me sleeve, an' me serviorite.
Then the lady as I 'ad fust met in the 'all
Who the other all called "The Dookess,"
She 'ands me a lovely gold watch, an' she ses:
"That's the prize for the best fancy dress,"
Arter supper us went ter the ballroom
An' I tried a dance as they called *"Pass-de-Quart,"* –
But I soon chucked it up, 'cause me old 'ob-nail boots
In the ladies' frocks kep' gettin' caught.
Then the Dookess, 'er ses: "Your *finance* 'as just come,"
An' a young gal in low hevenin' dress
Comes straight up ter me, – an' starts larfin', an ses:
"Well Percy, you do look a mess!"
Then she ses: "I 'ave just got ten thousand pounds
That was lef' me last year by me aunt, –
So now we'll get married next month, shall we dear?"
I ses: "No *love,* hus bloomin' well *shan't"*
So she ses: "Why what *reason* is there for delay?
The Pater no longer forbids," –
I ses: "There's *ten* reasons!" – "What are they?" she hasks,
I hanswers: "*One* wife an' *nine* kids!"
Then she ses: "What a bounder you are for a joke,
And you always so serious keep: –
Now come Percy love –" I ses: "Eh! Look 'ere miss,
I *ain't* 'Percy love' – *I'm the sweep!"*

Greatrex Newman and Fred Cecil

When you performed the poem could you hear the speaker's different voices? Did they sound differently? Did the different characters use different sorts of words?

Research and record

Now with a tape recorder, record as many different voices as you can of speakers who come from different parts of the country to where you live. You will be amazed at how many different speakers you can find in school and in your neighbourhood. Try interviewing them about the way they speak. Ask them to talk about the words they use which locals do not. Ask them to list some words that they feel they pronounce very differently from the way locals do and to explain to you how they pronounce them differently.

In a group, trace an outline map of Great Britain from an atlas. Play back your tape and try and record on the map the different words your subjects have told you about, where your subjects come from and, if you can, how their pronunciation is different.

LANGUAGE NOTE

The way in which you pronounce the words you speak is called your *accent*. The type of accent you have can depend on where you have lived most of your life. People from different countries speak with different accents, as do people from different parts of the same country.

Not only do people from different parts of the country pronounce words differently, they can use different forms of the same language. The vocabulary and grammar of this language form will be typical of one area only. This is called a *dialect*.

5 Language and life

Discuss

In groups, read the extract from *Where There's Life* by Kathleen Dayus. Make a performance reading, with one member of the group reading the storyline, and the others taking parts in the dialogue. The scene of the extract is set in 1913, one year before the First World War.

What examples of different forms of words and sentence patterns can you find? Look for:

▶ different forms from the ones you are used to – 'goo on' may not be the way you say 'go on'.
▶ different forms from Standard English – for example 'T'ain't' instead of 'It isn't'.
▶ evidence that the people speaking in the extract are working class – look at the forms of language and the details of their lives that the writer picks out.

The news soon went round the district about why Miss Louise had come to live there. Liza took care of that before I had a chance, but I didn't mind this; she was better at it than me. I was fetching a tin bowl of water from the tap in the yard when I heard Mum call out, 'Katie, fetch me a bucket of slack† before yer goo ter school.'

I was scared stiff of going down those cellar steps but Frankie wasn't around to do it so I had to do as I was told. As I was struggling down the yard with the full laden bucket a few minutes later a neighbour, Mrs Woods, saw me. I tried to walk past her but she caught hold of the bucket.

'We want yow in the wash'ouse,' she insisted. I followed, and on reaching the door I saw Mrs Jonesy, Mrs Phipps, Maggie and Mum, together with two or three more from the other yards, in animated conversation. It was cold and snowy outside so I squeezed in with them. They were chattering like a lot of parrots but I listened to what was said.

'Well fancy that.'

'I carn't believe it.'

'T'ain't true.'

Mum broke in decisively. 'It might be a good idea an' find out,' she said.

'It'd be betta than gooin' ter uncle's,' one said.

With this it dawned on me what they were talking about so I became more attentive.

'Well goo on then ask 'er,' said Mrs Woods.

'Well goo on then.' Mum shook me. 'Tell us. Is that the truth? Is she a money lender?'

'Yes Mum,' I told her.

'Right. That's all we want ter know. Yer can get off ter school now before yer late.' She spoke sharply and pushed me outside where it was snowing hard.

In school the girls kept whispering and turning round to look at me; Liza had told everyone. But it was not until we were in the playground that they could tackle me.

'Make way for Miss Louise,' they chorused, but I was not bothered by their sarcasm: it was the snowballs that some threw that mattered. I was alone; even Liza looked on as the snowballs rained down. I turned to run but slipped over, and that was too much even for my sister who came to my rescue and dared them to throw any more. They did not.

'What's wrong with 'em?' I cried. 'What 'ave I done?'

'I told 'em about you an' the money lender but I didn't know they were gooin' to snowball yer,' she said, pulling me to my feet.

I rather liked the name 'Louise' but not the

snowballs, and from that day on until I left school the girls who didn't like me called after me: 'There goes Miss Louise.' It was jealousy, I suppose; the fact that I had spotted a chance they had not, although I couldn't get over the suspicion that their reaction to me had something to do with how Liza had told the story.

When I returned home that afternoon I was surprised to find Dad already sitting in his chair by the fire.

'Aren't you at work, Dad?' I asked him.

'No I ain't,' he answered sharply, which was strange for him. 'An' where's yer Mum?'

She must have been upstairs because almost as if in answer to him we heard her heavy tread on the stairs. I could see the mood Dad was in and all I wanted to do was to make myself scarce before they started to quarrel.

'I don't want any tea Mum,' I called out quickly before she was down the stairs. 'Miss Louise will be waitin' for me.'

'What's all this about?' inquired Dad grumpily. 'What yer mean yer don't want any tea?'

'It's all right Sam, she's fetchin' errands fer the old lady that lives in the cottage.'

Dad stared at her hard before he replied. 'It seems to me that she's always over there.'

'I've told yer Sam,' snapped Mum, 'she's outa mischief, an' besides, it's one less ter feed.'

From *Where There's Life*, Kathleen Dayus

† Coal dust sold more cheaply than lump coal and was added to the lump coal to make it last longer.

'The word in language is half someone else's'

You have just been looking at an account of life in the slums of Birmingham in 1913. The words used by Mum, Liza, Mrs Phipps, Dad all come from the language of their community. They have a history, just like the words you researched in Module 1.

Research

Find out from your parents and grandparents some of the words they used as children. Do they use them now? Are they English words, or from another language? Are they local dialect words? What are they in Standard English? Make a chart showing your findings. Use a timeline to date the words used by your parents and grandparents, and to compare them with today's words.

If you cannot do that piece of research. . .

Using a large dictionary (the sort you will find in the library at school or your local public library), make a list of 50 words which have come into English in the last hundred years. Ask your other subject teachers for some help. Many of the new words in English come from science, technology and other languages.

Glasnost and **Perestroika** are very recent additions to English. Do you know what they mean? Which language do they come from?

'You don't mean it, do you?'

Discuss and write

With a partner, talk about the times when you find words difficult to understand, or when other people put pressure on you to use language the way they want you to.

Some examples of people not agreeing about each other's language might be:
▶ a teacher and pupil
▶ a police officer and a suspect
▶ two politicians from different parties
▶ a 'posh' child and a tough child
▶ a boy and a girl
▶ two people from different races
▶ parents and children.

Make a dialogue between two people who do not agree about the language each is using. Choose your words carefully to show their differences.

⑥ Home and school

Read and discuss

Home and school do not always mix. Read the extract from Leila Berg's *Look at Kids*.

HOW DO YOU SPEAK AT HOME? DO HOME AND SCHOOL LANGUAGE MIX?

In a South London school I sat down at a table with four seven-year-old girls. Another little girl came up to me – bringing a list of very neat and carefully written words to show me. They must have been copied off pictures on the wall. The first word was *yarn*. Truly.

'Do you know what this word is?' I asked her.

'Wool,' she said brightly.

The second word was *yacht*.

'And do you know what this is?' I said.

'Sailing boat,' she said brightly.

'Well, love,' I said, pulling her down next to me and putting my arm round her, 'it's really "yarn" and "yacht" . . . But never mind, you all tell me what are *important* words, and I'll write them all down.'

And without a second's hesitation, right round that table went 'ambulance' – 'dead' – 'dying' – 'nearly dead'. Now a slight pause. Then, quickly again, 'hospital' – 'doctors' – 'nurses'.

'Oh,' I said, 'has someone you

know died then?' A child on my right said, 'My Nan's died. Died on Tuesday. I saw her in her coffin. But I didn't go to the funeral. Our Linda went.'

'Who's Linda?' I said.

'Her big sister,' said her friend.

'Linda looks after us,' said the first child.

'Where's your Mum then?' I asked.

'She ran away.'

'Cos she couldn't stand the row,' said her friend.

'And where's your Dad?'

'He's dead.'

All this completely matter-of-fact. Yarn . . . yachts . . . John, see the boats . . . And the important words are 'dead' – 'dying' – 'nearly dead'.

I think what I find most extraordinary of all is that if I tell people this they think I am being depressing.

From *Look at Kids*, Leila Berg

In your groups discuss the extract. Focus on:
▶ What are your feelings about it? Does it depress you?
▶ How does it show differences between school work and experience of real life at home?
▶ Identify the words which give you clues to your answers.

In groups make lists of your ten most important words. Using the messenger/reporter system, give the lists from each group to the messengers. They should check the lists to see if the same words occur in the different lists. The information should be presented to the class, using the blackboard.

Discuss

After listening to the results of your group work, discuss how you think home and school could be made closer, so that your work at school and your life at home did not clash. Look at:
▶ What is important at home and at school?
▶ What are the differences in language at home and school?
(Look back at Module 1 for some ideas to get you started.)

Homespeak and schoolspeak

Read and discuss

With a partner read the extract on p. 74 from *Tess of the d'Urbervilles*, by Thomas Hardy.

Make a list of the words you do not know. Find out what they mean by reading the passage again. For example, if you do not know what 'fess' means, read on – the clues are in the extract. Mrs Durbeyfield thinks that her husband, Tess's father, has had some good news. Why could 'fess' not mean 'sad'?

If there are any words you do not understand after your second reading, note them down and look them up in a large dictionary.

Discuss the times when you think Tess would not know which dialect to use. Are there any times when you use your local dialects?

'Well, I'm glad you've come,' her mother said, as soon as the last note had passed out of her. 'I want to go and fetch your father; but what's more'n that, I want to tell 'ee what have happened. Y'll be fess enough, my poppet, when th'st know!' (Mrs. Durbeyfield habitually spoke the dialect; her daughter, who had passed the Sixth Standard in the National School under a London-trained mistress, spoke two languages: the dialect at home, more or less; ordinary English abroad and to persons of quality.)

'Since I've been away?' Tess asked.

'Ay!'

'Had it anything to do with father's making such a mommet of himself in thik carriage this afternoon? Why did 'er? I felt inclined to sink into the ground with shame!'

'That wer all a part of the larry! We've been found to be the greatest gentlefolk in the whole country—reaching all back long before Oliver Grumble's time—to the days of the Pagan Turks—with monuments, and vaults, and crests, and 'scutcheons, and the Lord knows what all. In Saint Charles's days we was made Knights o' the Royal Oak, our real name being d'Urberville! . . . Don't that make your bosom plim? 'Twas on this account that your father rode home in the vlee; not because he'd been drinking, as people supposed.'

'I'm glad of that. Will it do us any good, mother?'

'O yes! 'Tis thoughted that great things may come o't. No doubt a mampus of volk of our own rank will be down here in their carriages as soon as 'tis known. Your father learnt it on his way hwome from Shaston, and he has been telling me the whole pedigree of the matter.'

'Where is father now?' asked Tess suddenly.

From *Tess of the d'Urbervilles*,
Thomas Hardy

7 Who killed the bears?

Read aloud and discuss

In groups read the story of the bears aloud. Each member of the group should take a turn with each verse. Discuss the problems of reading this dialect poem so that it sounds 'right'. Focus points:

▶ Look at the many different dialect forms such as 'thic', 'vram', 'dree' and 'exin'.
▶ Find out what all the dialect words you identify mean in Standard English.
▶ Would the poem be better or worse in Standard English?

WHO KILLED THE BEARS?

Hast ever 'eard o' Ruardean?
Thic place be'ind the 'ill
Where, if thouse like vresh air in chunks
Then thee const 'ave thee vill.

Vram thic there bank on zunny day
Thouse look right inta Wales
An' there yunt much 'tween there an' thee
Ta stop them south-west gales.

Well, thic there view, though p'rhaps as fine
As any thou const name
Yunt why them chaps as live up there
'Ave earned a place in fame.

Thay don't appear to be bad blokes
Thay don't put on no airs
But, years agoo, ar zo tis zed
Them chaps thay killed zum bears.

Zum vurriners vram 'cross the sea
Were 'awkin' round the lanes
An' thay 'ad got zum bears wi' um
Draggin' round on chains.

Well, zum vool started up a yarn
That bears 'ad killed a lad
An' thic tale gettin's round the place
Zoon got the volks 'alf mad.

Wi' sticks an' stwuns an' iron bars
Brick-bats an' chunks of 'ood
Dree parts the village zet off out
Ta stop them bears vor good.

Them vurriners thay chased an' byut
An' rolled um in the mud
An' them there bears thay laid out vlat
An' left um there, stwun jud.

Well, that's the tale as I were tawld
An' I could never tell
Why, each time thouse remind um on't,
Them chaps da kick up "Merry Andrew"

Thay be zo touchy 'bout it all
That vram thic day till now
If thou dost only whisper "bears"
Thouse exin vor a row.

I used ta laugh about it once
An' zed I 'ad me doubts
Zo, one night, back zum years agoo
I went there ta vind out.

I drapped inta the public bar
O' thic there place, the Bell
'Bout dozen chaps were drinkin' there
As near as I could tell.

I zized um up both one an' all
An though they looked bit rough
There wasn't nern as big as I
Thay didn't look that tough.

I got my back agen a wall
An' turned an' faced their stares
Then, gettin' ready vor the fun
I exed, "Who killed the bears?"

Vor 'alf a minute time stood still
Thay looked at I each one
I started ta let out a laugh
An' then the fun begun.

I've 'ad zum fights when I were young
'Cos I be Vorest barn
But when I think what 'appened then
I vind my blood run warm.

I spread my vit an' clenched my tith
An' ladled round I plenty
But vor each one I gid awoy
I back I gathered twenty.

This lasted vor a goodish bit
It zeemed an hour ar more
An' never 'ave I bin zo glad
Ta come back droo a door.

'Tis true, thay opened 'im vor I
An' I come droo yud vust
An' then thay stood an' looked at I
As I rolled in the dust.

Thay stood an' watched I quiut
As I scrambled to my vit
And one, 'im tossed my 'at to I
Another, my top tith.

READ A DIALECT POEM. ENJOY ITS DIFFERENCE, AND ITS HUMOUR. MAKE A PLAYSCRIPT FROM ITS STORY LINE.

I went back wum a wiser mon
I'd paid vor all my fun
I never stopped ta look be'ind
Nar never went agyun.

Well, that were many years agoo
And them there days be done
Thay zay it yunt like that there now
But that's as maybe son.

If thou bist ver up thic road
An' veel thouse like zum fun
Thou exe um who t'was killed the bears
But, Mister—TAKE A GUN!!

Dennis Potter, a writer who lived
in the Forest of Dean, knew the
story of the bears and made a
play from it. It's your turn now!

Discuss and write

In groups, brainstorm the main points of the story about the bears.

Make a web diagram of the plot for a play using the bears story.
You will need:
▶ an opening scene
▶ some scenes between the 'foreigners' and the locals
▶ some scenes in which the 'vool' (fool) tells the story about the bears killing a boy
▶ a scene, or scenes, where the locals are ashamed at killing the bears (your chance to make up some characters here)
▶ the big fight
▶ the scene where the storyteller looks back at his fight and what he thinks – who could this scene be with?

Make some notes for each scene, then decide on the one which you like best. Write a script for this scene. Look back at Module 3 to check on writing dialogues and scripts, p. 48.

You could try writing some of the dialogue in the Forest of Dean dialect, or your own local dialect.

⑧ Crime and punishment

Read and discuss

With a partner, read the extract from *London's Underworld*. The author, Henry Mayhew, investigated the lives of criminals and poor people in Victorian London.

Discuss the way the burglar tells his story. Focus points:
▶ What is the point of view? Is it matter of fact, or gloating?
▶ Is the story told sensationally? Find some evidence for your answers.
▶ Why did the burglar become tired of country life? Use your imagination here.

"At the back of the premises we cut our way into the passage, and, according to the directions given to us in the plan that had been drawn, we had to go up to the second floor, and enter a door there. We found nothing in the room we had entered but neckties and collars, which would not have paid us for bringing them away. We then had to work our way through a back wall before we got into the apartment where the silks were stored. They cut through the brick wall cleverly. We had all taken rum to steady our nerve before we went to work.

"We had gone up the wrong staircase, which was the cause of our having to cut through the wall. There was only one man that slept in the house, and he was in a room on the basement. We at last, after much labour and delay, got into the right room, pressed the bolt back, and found we could get away by the other staircase. We got silks, handkerchiefs, and other drapery goods, and had about £18 each after disposing of them—which was about two-thirds of their value. We had a cab to carry away the things for us to the 'fence' who received them.

GET INTO THE HEAD OF AN OLD FASHIONED BURGLAR. PREVENT CRIME! BE A TABLOID REPORTER.

"We went to another burglary at Islington, and made an entrance into the house, but were disturbed, and ran away over several walls and gardens.

"We attempted a third burglary in the City. As usual we had a plan of it through a man that had been at work there, who put it up for us. This was a shop in which there were a great many Geneva watches. We got in at this time by the back window, and went upstairs. We were told that the master went away at 1 o'clock. On this occasion he had remained later than usual, looking over his business books. On seeing us he made an outcry and struggled with us. Assistance came immediately. Two policemen ran up to the house. In the scramble with the man in the house we tried to make for the door. The police could not get in, as the door was bolted. We were determined to make a rush out. I undid the chain and drew back the bolt. I got away, and had fled along two or three streets, when I was stunned by a man who carried a closed umbrella. Hearing the cry of 'Stop thief!' he drew out the umbrella, and I fell as I was running. I was thereupon taken back by one of the policemen, and found both of the others in custody. We were committed for trial next day, and sent to Newgate in the meantime for detention.

"My former convictions were not brought against me. My two companions had been previously at Newgate, and were sentenced the one to ten years' and the other to seven years' penal servitude, while I got eighteen months' imprisonment in Holloway Prison. I was the younger of the party, and had no convictions. I never engaged in burglary after this. At this time I was twenty-two or twenty-three years of age.

"I came out of prison in 1853, and was unnerved for some time though my health was good. This was the effect of the solitary confinement.

"When I came out, I wrote home for the first time since I had been in London, and received a letter back stating that my father was dead after an illness of several years, and that I was to come home, adding that if I required money, they would send it me. Besides, there were several things they were to give me, according to my father's wishes.

"I went home, and had thoughts of stopping there. My mother was not in such good position as I expected, the property left by my grandfather having gone to a distant relative at my father's death. She was and is still in receipt of a weekly sum from the old Wesleyan fund for the benefit of the widows of ministers.

"I went home in the end of 1853, and had the full intention of stopping there, though I promised to Sally to be back in a few weeks. I soon got tired of the country life, though my relations were very kind to me, and after remaining seven weeks at home, came back to London again about the commencement of 1854, and commenced working by myself at stealing watches and breast-pins. I did not work at ladies' pockets unless I had comrades beside me. I went and mingled in the crowds by myself.

"In the end of 1854 I got another six months' imprisonment at Hick's Hall police court, and was sent to Coldbath Fields, and was told that if I ever come again before the criminal authorities, I would be transported.

From *London's Underworld*, Henry Mayhew

Discuss

In groups, discuss the length of prison sentences imposed on the burglars. Focus on:
▶ whether it is right or wrong to send someone to prison for ten years for burglary
▶ whether being in prison makes criminals better people.

Make a list, in each group, of the ways you would prevent crime today and help criminals to reform. Use the messenger/reporter system to share the results among the class.

Discuss and write

Imagine you are reporters for a tabloid newspaper, like the *Mirror* or the *Sun*. Take the burglar's story up to 'twenty-three years of age' and rewrite it for today. Talk about:
▶ the point of view you want to create
▶ how sensational you want to make it
▶ how your choice of words and phrases affects your readers.

9 Strong feelings

Read and discuss

The poem below comes from Anglo-Saxon England. It tells how a woman feels when she is kept far away from her husband. He is in another country.

Read the poem carefully. With a partner, talk about:

▶ your first reactions to the poem
▶ words and ideas you do not understand at first
▶ patterns you can see in the poem – for example repeated words, parts of words, letters
▶ images which you think express feelings strongly
▶ words, phrases or lines you specially like/dislike
▶ how you would recommend the poem to another reader.

I have wrought these words together out of a wryed existence,
the heart's tally, telling of
the grief I have undergone from girlhood upwards,
old and new, and now more than ever;
for I have never not had some new sorrow,
some fresh affliction to fight against.
The first was my lord's leaving his people here:
crossed crests. To what country I knew not,
wondered where, awoke unhappy.
I left, fared any road, friendless, an outcast,
sought any service to staunch the lack of him.

Then his kinsmen ganged, began to think
thoughts they did not speak, of splitting the wedlock,
so – estranged, alienated – we lived each
alone, a long way apart; how I longed for him!
In his harshness he had brought me here;
and in these parts there were few friendly minded,
worth trusting.

   Trouble in the heart now:
I saw the bitterness, the bound mind
of my matched man, mourning browe,
mirk in his mood, murder in his thoughts.

▶ SEE HOW YOU CAN PUT STRONG FEELINGS INTO A POEM. MAKE A POEM WITH YOU[R] STRONG FEELINGS.

Our lips had smiled to swear hourly
that nothing should split us – save dying –
nothing else. All that has changed;
it is now as if it never had been,
our friendship. I feel in the wind
That the man dearest to me detests me.
I was banished to this knoll, knotted by woods
to live in a den dug beneath an oak.
Old is this earthen room; it eats at my heart.

I see the thorns up there in thick coverts
on the banks that baulk these black hollows:
not a gay dwelling. Here the grief bred
by lordlack preys on me. Some lovers in this world
live dear to each other, lie warm together
at day's beginning: I go by myself
about these earth caves under the oak tree.
Here I must sit the summer day through,
here weep out the woes of exile,
the hardships heaped upon me. My heart shall never
suddenly sail into slack water,
all the longings of a lifetime unanswered.

May grief and bitterness blast the mind
of that young man! May his mind ache
behind his smiling face! May a flock of sorrows
choke his chest! He would change his tune
if he lived alone in a land of exile
far from his folk.
    Where my friend is stranded
frost crusts the cracked cliff-face,
grey waves grind the shingle.
The mind cannot bear in such a bleak place very much grief.
    He remembers too often
less grim surroundings. Sorrow follows
this too long wait for one who is estranged.

Writing

Look again at the ways in which the writer of the poem shows us the feelings of the woman on her own. Think about **your** feelings.

▶ Identify the people, places, animals, things or events which you feel strongly about.
▶ Brainstorm some words and phrases for those feelings.
▶ Try putting your ideas into a sequence for a poem.
▶ Look at the line lengths, and the rhythms.
▶ Have you made up some strong images for your feelings?
▶ Draft the first version, then leave it for a while.
▶ Come back to your first version, change anything you need to, to make it work for you.
▶ Check the spelling and punctuation.
▶ Decide how you will present it. Will it be best handwritten or word-processed? Will it have illustrations?
▶ Ask your teacher to help make a class display of your finished poems, under the heading 'Strong Feelings'.

10 Spirit of place

Research

Imagine you have just become the tourist officer for the place where you live. You need to find some interesting facts about your area. Ask your history and geography teachers for help, and see what you can find out from your local reference library. Think about some of these points:

G.N.R.

SKEGNESS IS SO BRACING

▶ When did people first begin to live in your area? Check on the names of local places like villages, or names of streets.
▶ What is your area like? Town, or countryside, or city?
▶ Where is it and how can you get there from other places? Is there an airport, a motorway, or a railway station?
▶ What details about the area do you need to put in your list, to make it clear to tourists what there is to see and do?
▶ Are there any interesting geographical features, like hills, rivers, seaside, underground streams, caves?
▶ Are there any interesting man-made features, especially buildings or parks?
▶ What jobs do people in the area do?

Make a list of your results. Then . . .

Discuss

In groups, share your sets of facts. Make a short audio-tape which introduces your area to prospective tourists. Keep these points in focus:
▶ The purpose of the tape is to attract tourists.
▶ Tourists need something to do, to see, places to eat and drink.
▶ If the weather is bad, they need somewhere to go. What entertainment is there?
▶ Highlight the really unusual features of the area. It might be interesting for its history, its industry, its legends, its geography or its local people.

▶ Choose your words carefully. You have to persuade your listeners to come to your part of the country.
▶ Explain very clearly about places and things which tourists would not know.

Produce your tape and select the best one by a class vote. You could send it to the local tourist board for their comments.

USE YOUR SPEAKING AND LISTENING SKILLS TO MAKE A TOURIST ATTRACTION TAPE.

COMMERCIAL ROAD
WEST PARK ROAD
COMMERCIAL ROAD
WEST MARLANDS ROAD
ABOVE BAR STREET
PARK WALK
East Park
EAST PARK TERRACE
ST ANDREWS ROAD
College of Further Education
Mountbatten Theatre
College of Further Education
NORTHAM ROAD
WYNDHAM PLACE
HAVELOCK ROAD
Mayflower Theatre
WEST PARK ROAD
Civic Centre Guildhall Library Art Gallery
Buses only
BLECHYNDEN TERRACE
Police Station Law Courts
ABC Cinema
AA
NEW ROAD
PALMERSTON ROAD
NORTH FRONT
WINTON
ST
COSSACK
GREEN
BROAD
GREEN
KINGSWAY
GOLDEN GROVE
Southampton Station
WESTERN ESPLANADE
CIVIC CENTRE ROAD
Palmerston Park
Kingsland Square Market
Pedestrians only
MANCHESTER ST
SUSSEX ROAD
SOUTH FRONT
JAMES STREET
Driver Education Centre
PORTLAND TERRACE
OGLE ROAD
Odeon Cinema
PORTLAND STREET
P.O.
POUND TREE ROAD
Houndwell Park
Hoglands
ST MARYS PLACE
ST MARYS STREET
COLEMAN STREET
WEST QUAY ROAD
ABOVE BAR STREET
WALK
VINCENTS
Buses only
HANOVER BUILDINGS
HOUNDWELL PLACE
CHAPEL ST
Technical College
City Industrial Park
Arundel or Wind Whistle Tower
BARGATE ST
Bargate
BUILDINGS
YORK
Polymood Tower
COOK
St Marys Church
CHAPEL ROAD
Catchcold Tower
EAST STREET
East Street Centre
EAST STREET
LIME STREET
EVANS ST
CANAL WALK
ORCHARD LANE
KING STREET
MARSH LANE
CENTRAL BRIDGE
HERBERT WALKER AVENUE
Central Swimming Baths
Town Walls
UPPER BUGLE STREET
SIMNEL ST
CASTLE WAY
HIGH STREET
EASTGATE ST
OF THE WALLS
QUEENS WAY
Holy Rood Church
CHARLES STREET
DUKE ST
RICHMOND ST COLLEGE
CENTRAL BRIDGE
Cattle Market
Western Docks (Berths 108–101)
Mayflower Park
N
Tudor House Museum
West Gate
St Michaels Church
BUGLE STREET
BACK STREET
H.P.O.
ORIENTAL TERRACE
BRITON STREET
BERNARD STREET
BRUNSWICK SQUARE
ORCHARD PLACE
OXFORD STREET
LATIMER STREET
JOHN STREET
TERMINUS TERRACE
ST STREET
Hall of Aviation
BBC South Television & BBC Radio Solent
Maritime Museum
FRENCH STREET
PORTERS LA
WINKLE STREET
BACK OF THE WALLS
LWR CANAL WALK
ORCHARD PLACE
QUEENS TERRACE
Queen's Park
CANUTE ROAD
BOUNDARY ROAD
Central Southampton
TOWN QUAY
God's House
God's Gate
God's House Tower
PLATFORM ROAD
WEST ROAD
CUNARD ROAD
CENTRAL ROAD
OLD ROAD
MELBURY RD
Future Development
Landing Stage for Cowes Ferry Boats and Hydrofoil
Hythe Passenger Ferry Terminal
Town Quay

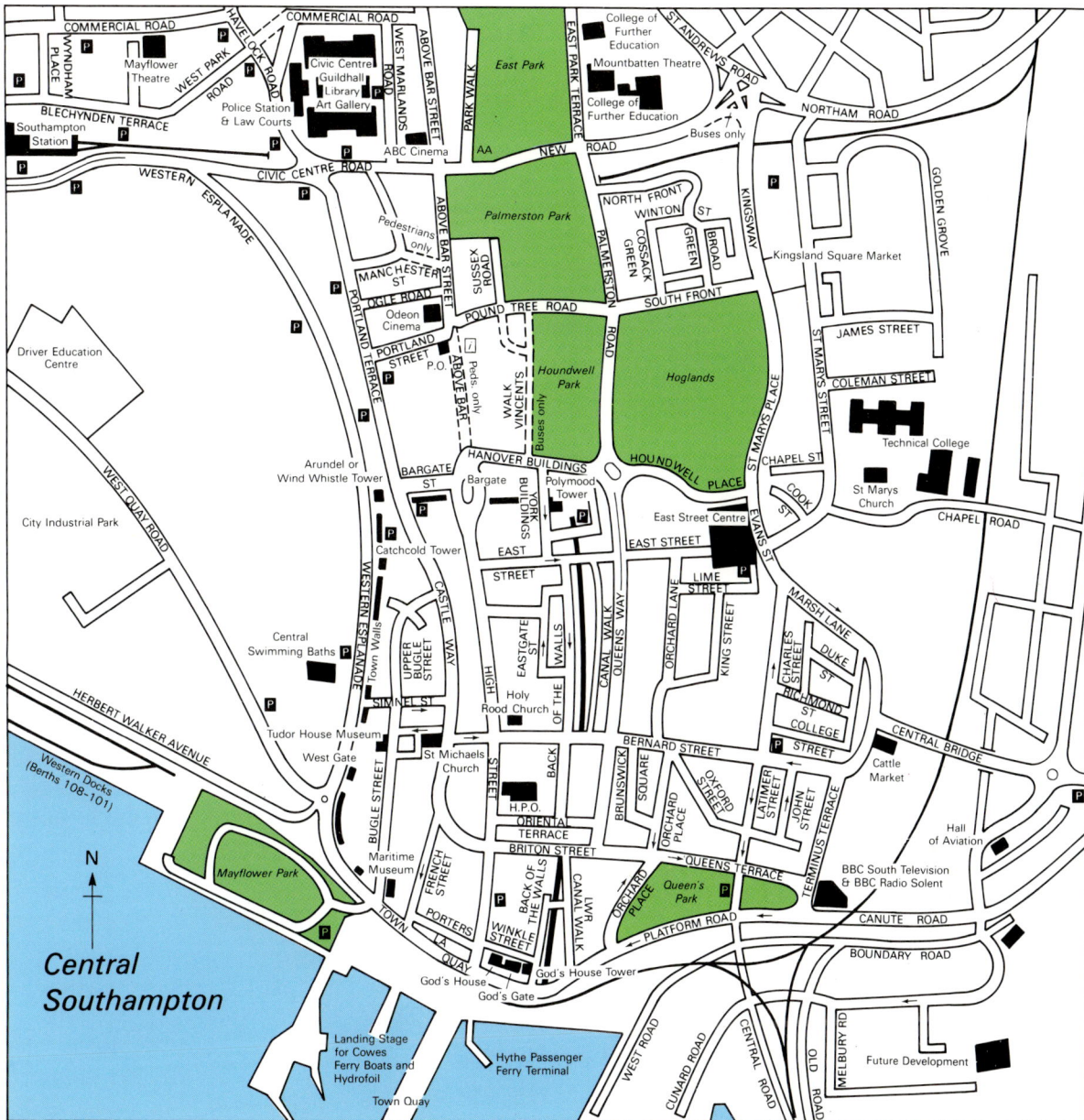

Discuss and improvise

With a partner, look at the map of central Southampton. If you do not know where Southampton is, find out with the help of a map of England.

One of you should take the role of stranger to the town. The other should be a local who knows the area well. The stranger is at the Driver Education Centre, and wants to go to BBC South Television.

In role, improvise a conversation which enables the stranger to get to his/her destination.

▶ If you are the stranger, think about the questions you need to ask – for example, the landmarks to look for, or traffic problems such as one-way streets or road works.

▶ If you are the local, you need to make all the details clear to the stranger – for example, road names, landmarks, dangerous junctions.

▶ Stick to the facts which are on the map.

When you have improvised the situation, reverse roles. This time the stranger is at the College of Further Education, and wants to find God's House Tower.

Building words

Research

With a partner look closely at a map of your area. Focus on the names of the streets, the landmarks, the villages, the districts of the town or city.

▶ What do they mean?
▶ Where do the words come from – which language?
▶ How are the words built up?

Look at the example below for some ideas about place names.

LLANFAIRPWLLGWYNGYLLGOGERYCHWYRNDROBWLLLLANTYSILIOGOGOGOCH
ST MARYS CHURCH IN THE HOLLOW OF THE WHITE HAZEL NEAR TO THE RAPID WHIRLPOOL OF LLANTYSILIO OF THE RED CAVE

The picture above shows the station sign from the place in Britain which has the longest name. This is in Anglesey in Wales. Have a go at reading it aloud! (The 'Ll-' is pronounced 'Cl-'). The other places shown on this page have names which are easier to say, but are just as interesting. It is easy to see where a name like Blackpool or Cambridge comes from; we may have to think harder or do some investigation to find the meanings of other place names.

The first people to settle in Britain were mostly farmers and they often named places after local landmarks. They picked out the things which were important to them such as rivers, hills and fields, or named places after the people who lived there. With a little practice you can soon learn to identify the different parts of place names and what they mean.

Sometimes there are different words in different parts of the country for the same thing, so a name may also help you to guess whereabouts in the country the place is. The Old English word for valley is 'dene', this gives us villages called Dean or Deane; it can also appear as '-den' on the end of a name, such as Haslingden (valley of hazels). The Danes called a valley 'dale' so in Yorkshire, where many Vikings settled, there are lots of names with 'dale' in them – Nidderdale (valley of the river Nidd), Wensleydale (valley by Wendel's wood). The Gaelic word for valley is 'cwm'; this was the same as 'combe' in Old English. There are several places in Britain called Combe or Coombe, and many places which have '-combe' or

'Com-' as part of them. For example Withycombe, which means valley full of willows (withy is an old word for willow tree) and Ilfracombe, which means 'valley of Alfred's people'. Many places in Wales have 'cwm' as part of them.

Because most of the early settlers were farmers many of the place names they gave have 'field' in them, so Stanfield was a 'stony field'. Trees were also important to them and the Old English word for a wood gives us 'leigh' (also spelt 'ley' or 'leah') which is found as part of many place names. They often had to clear away trees to make their fields. The names they left behind give us a clue as to what trees they were – Oakley and Ashley are clear enough; there was a birch wood at Berkeley and brooms at Bramley.

From *Beginnings*, Sue Benton

Words come into English from many languages. Sometimes there are some very clear patterns which you will recognise as you spend the next few terms at school.

Research

As you learn new subjects, put into your logs some words beginning with these prefixes. Look back at Module 1, p. 6, if you have forgotten about prefixes.

Ante	mini	pseudo
anti	mis	semi
auto	mono	sub
bi	multi	super
co	neo	trans
de	out	ultra
dis	over	under
fore	pan	uni
hyper	poly	
mal	pro	

You will meet suffixes in Book Two.

Discuss

Imagine you had the chance to create your own place to live. You do not have to worry about money when you think about this. Prepare some notes for a short talk which you are going to give on the local radio station and then as a class make an audio-tape called 'My Place'.

Ask your teacher to help you decide the order of the talks.

How do you read?

Introduction

On pp. 22–3 we looked at the variety of texts we read and how those texts differ from each other. In this module we will be looking at the process of reading – that is *how* we read. You will have the chance to think about the way you read novels, poems and information texts and you will be given the chance to practise your reading skills.

1 Reading pictures

Spot the clues

We saw in Module 2: Reading that we are surrounded by different types of reading material and we are sometimes reading without even being aware of it. We are also surrounded by pictures of different sorts and as we grow up we learn to read them too.

It will help us to understand how we read, if we first try a bit of detective work on a picture.

Reflect

Look at the picture carefully. Work out as much as you can about the character you see and what is happening.

EVERY PICTURE TELLS A STORY. CAN YOU WORK OUT THE STORY IN THIS ONE?

Now compare the conclusions you have come to with another person. Show each other where your ideas came from.

Which of the following aspects told you most about the person in the picture. Put them in order of helpfulness: most helpful first; least helpful last:

▶ actions
▶ dress
▶ expression
▶ position
▶ build
▶ possessions.

Now think about the way you make judgements about people you meet for the first time in real life. Are there any things about them that influence you that a picture cannot show? If you can think of any, list them.

2 Reading stories 1

Using the clues

By looking at the picture in the first unit of this module you have probably worked out for yourselves that in pictures we get important clues about the people in them from the various aspects of their appearance, their actions, what they own and from the settings we find them in. Before we make up our mind about such people in real life, however, we would probably like to speak to them. We may even like to hear from other people what they think about them.

When we are reading we use all these sorts of clues.

Read

Here is your chance to play detective with a real story by Jan Mark.

As you read this story, you will meet two characters called Mike and Ruth Dixon. Try to picture them in your mind. The writer will provide you with lots of clues about them. Your job as a reader is to be like a detective and to pick up these clues to build a picture of them in your mind.

Send Three and Fourpence
We are Going to a Dance

Mike and Ruth Dixon got on well enough, but not so well that they wanted to walk home from school together. Ruth would not have minded, but Mike, who was two classes up, preferred to amble along with his friends so that he usually arrived a long while after Ruth did.

Ruth was leaning out of the kitchen window when he came in through the side gate, kicking a brick.

'I've got a message for you,' said Mike. 'From school. Miss Middleton wants you to go and see her tomorrow before assembly, and take a dead frog.'

'What's she want *me* to take a dead frog for?' said Ruth. 'She's not my teacher. I haven't got a dead frog.'

'How should I know?' Mike let himself in. 'Where's Mum?'

'Round Mrs Todd's. Did she really say a dead frog? I mean, really say it?'

'Derek told me to tell you. It's nothing to do with me.'

Ruth cried easily. She cried now. 'I bet she never. You're pulling my leg.'

'I'm not, and you'd better do it. She said it was important – Derek said – and you know what a rotten old temper she's got,' said Mike, feelingly.

'But why me? It's not fair.' Ruth leaned her head on the window-sill and wept in earnest. 'Where'm I going to find a dead frog?'

'Well, you can peel them off the road sometimes, when they've been run over. They go all dry and flat, like pressed flowers,' said Mike. He did think it a trifle unreasonable to demand dead frogs from little girls, but Miss Middleton *was* unreasonable. Everyone knew that. 'You could start a pressed frog collection,' he said.

Ruth sniffed fruitily. 'What do you think Miss'll do if I don't get one?'

'She'll go barmy, that's what,' said Mike. 'She's barmy anyway,' he said. 'Nah, don' start howling again. Look, I'll go down the ponds after tea. I know there's frogs there because I saw the spawn, back at Easter.'

'But those frogs are alive. She wants a dead one.'

'I dunno. Perhaps we could get it put to sleep or something, like Mrs Todd's Tibby was. And don't tell Mum. She doesn't like me down the ponds and she won't let us have frogs indoors. Get an old box with a lid and leave it on the rockery, and I'll put old Froggo in it when I come home. *And stop crying*!'

After Mike had gone out Ruth found the box that her summer sandals had come in. She poked air holes in the top and furnished it with damp grass and a tin full of water. Then she left it on the rockery with a length of darning wool so that Froggo could be fastened down safely until morning. It was only possible to imagine Froggo alive; all tender and green and saying croak-croak. She could not think of him dead and flat and handed over to Miss Middleton, who definitely must have gone barmy. Perhaps Mike or Derek had been wrong about the dead part. She hoped they had.

She was in the bathroom, getting ready for bed, when Mike came home. He looked round the door and stuck up his thumbs.

'Operation Frog successful. Over and out.'

'Wait. Is he . . . alive?'

'Shhh. Mum's in the hall. Yes.'

'What's he like?'

'Sort of frog-shaped. Look, I've got him; O.K.? I'm going down now.'

'Is he green?'

'No. More like that pork pie that went mouldy on top. Good night!'

Mike had hidden Froggo's dungeon under the front hedge, so all Ruth had to do next morning was scoop it up as she went out of the gate. Mike had left earlier with his friends, so she paused for a moment to introduce herself. She tapped quietly on the lid. 'Hullo?'

There was no answering cry of croak-croak. Perhaps he *was* dead. Ruth felt a tear coming and raised the lid a fraction at one end. There was a scrabbling noise and at the other end of the box she saw something small and alive, crouching in the grass.

'Poor Froggo,' she whispered through the air holes. 'I won't let her kill you, I promise,' and she continued on her way to school feeling brave and desperate, and ready to protect Froggo's life at the cost of her own.

The school hall was in the middle of the building and classrooms opened off it. Miss Middleton had Class 3

this year, next to the cloakroom. Ruth hung up her blazer, untied the wool from Froggo's box, and went to meet her doom. Miss Middleton was arranging little stones in an aquarium on top of the bookcase, and jerked her head when Ruth knocked, to show that she should come in.

'I got him, Miss,' said Ruth, holding out the shoe box in trembling hands.

'What, dear?' said Miss Middleton, up to her wrists in water-weed.

'Only he's not dead and I won't let you kill him!' Ruth cried, and swept off the lid with a dramatic flourish. Froggo, who must have been waiting for this, sprung out, towards Miss Middleton, landed with a clammy sound on that vulnerable place between the collar bones, and slithered down inside Miss Middleton's blouse.

Miss Middleton taught Nature Study. She was not afraid of little damp creatures, but she was not

expecting Froggo. She gave a squawk of alarm and jumped backwards. The aquarium skidded in the opposite direction; took off; shattered against a desk. The contents broke over Ruth's new sandals in a tidal wave, and Lily the goldfish thrashed about in a shallow puddle on the floor. People came running with mops and dustpans. Lily Fish was taken out by the tail to recover in the cloakroom sink. Froggo was arrested while trying to leave Miss Middleton's blouse through the gap between two buttons, and put back in his box with a weight on top in case he made another dash for freedom.

Ruth, crying harder than she had ever done in her life, was sent to stand outside the Headmaster's room, accused of playing stupid practical jokes; and cruelty to frogs.

ABOUT THE SORTS OF CLUES TO LOOK FOR.

Sir looked rather as if he had been laughing, but it seemed unlikely, under the circumstances, and Ruth's eyes were so swollen and tear-filled that she couldn't see clearly. He gave her a few minutes to dry out and then said,

'This isn't like you, Ruth. Whatever possessed you to go throwing frogs at poor Miss Middleton? And poor frog, come to that.'

'She told me to bring her a frog,' said Ruth, stanching another tear at the injustice of it all. 'Only she wanted a dead one, and I couldn't find a dead one, and I couldn't kill Froggo. I won't kill him,' she said, remembering her vow on the way to school.

'Miss Middleton says she did not ask you to bring her a frog, or kill her a frog. She thinks you've been very foolish and unkind,' said Sir, 'and I think you are not telling the truth. Now . . .'

'Mike told me to,' said Ruth.

'Your brother? Oh, come now.'

'He did. He said Miss Middleton wanted me to go to her before assembly with a dead frog and I did, only it

Has Mike played a practical joke on his sister Ruth or not? Is there some other possible explanation?

If you were the Head investigating this situation you would have to play detective. Before you punished Mike you would have to be confident that he had the **motive** and the **opportunity** to trick his sister and you would then have to find some **evidence** to prove that he did it.

Use this page from a detective's notebook to help you build your case for or against Mike.

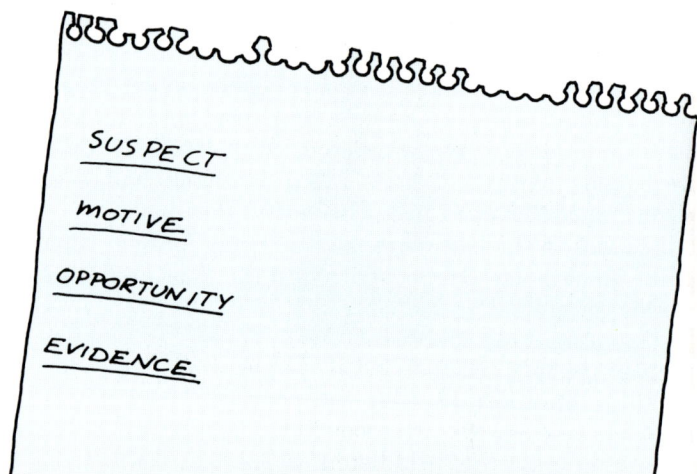

wasn't dead and I won't!'

'Ruth! Don't grizzle. No one is going to murder your frog, but we must get this nonsense sorted out.' Sir opened his door and called to a passer-by, 'Tell Michael Dixon that I want to see him at once, in my office.'

Mike arrived, looking wary. He had heard the crash and kept out of the way, but a summons from Sir was not to be ignored.

'Come in, Michael,' said Sir. 'Now, why did you tell your sister that Miss Middleton wanted her to bring a dead frog to school?'

'It wasn't me,' said Mike. 'It was a message from Miss Middleton.'

'Miss Middleton told you?'

'No, Derek Bingham told me. She told him to tell me – I suppose,' said Mike, sulkily. He scowled at Ruth. All her fault.

'Then you'd better fetch Derek Bingham here right away. We're going to get to the bottom of this.'

Derek arrived. He too had heard the crash.

SUSPECT

MOTIVE

OPPORTUNITY

EVIDENCE

Read and discuss

Now compare your case with your partner's. Would you punish Mike on the evidence you have gathered so far, or do you think he is innocent?

Do you think there might be some other possible explanation?

Now read on.

'Come in, Derek,' said Sir. 'I understand that you told Michael here some tarradiddle about his sister. You let him think it was a message from Miss Middleton, didn't you?'

'Yes, well . . .' Derek shuffled. 'Miss Middleton didn't tell *me*. She told, er, someone, and they told me.'

'Who was this someone?'

Derek turned all noble and stood up straight and pale. 'I can't remember, Sir.'

'Don't let's have any heroics about sneaking, Derek, or I shall get very *cross*.'

Derek's nobility ebbed rapidly. 'It was Tim Hancock, Sir. He said Miss Middleton wanted Ruth Dixon to bring her a dead dog before assembly.'

'A dead *dog*?'

'Yes Sir.'

'Didn't you think it a bit strange that Miss Middleton should ask Ruth for a dead dog, Derek?'

'I thought she must have one, Sir.'

'But why should Miss Middleton want it?'

'Well, she does do Nature Study,' said Derek.

'Go and fetch Tim,' said Sir.

Tim had been playing football on the field when the aquarium went down. He came in with an innocent smile which wilted when he saw what was waiting for him.

'Sir?'

'Would you mind repeating the message that you

gave Derek yesterday afternoon?'

'I told him Miss Middleton wanted Sue Nixon to bring her a red sock before assembly,' said Tim. 'It was important.'

'Red sock? Sue Nixon?' said Sir. He was beginning to look slightly wild-eyed. 'Who's Sue Nixon? There's no one in this school called Sue Nixon.'

'I don't know any of the girls, Sir,' said Tim.

'Didn't you think a red sock was an odd thing to ask for?'

'I thought she was bats, Sir.'

'Sue Nixon?'

'No Sir. Miss Middleton, Sir,' said truthful Tim.

Sir raised his eyebrows. 'But why did you tell Derek?'

'I couldn't find anyone else, Sir. It was late.'

'But why Derek?'

'I had to tell someone or I'd have got into trouble,' said Tim, virtuously.

'You are in trouble,' said Sir. 'Michael, ask Miss Middleton to step in here for a moment, please.'

Miss Middleton, frog-ridden, looked round the door. 'I'm sorry to bother you again,' said Sir, 'but it seems that Tim thinks you told him that one Sue Nixon was to bring you a red sock before assembly.'

'Tim!' said Miss Middleton, very shocked. 'That's a naughty fib. I never told you any such thing.'

'Oh Sir,' said Tim. 'Miss didn't tell me. It was Pauline Bates done that.'

'Did that. I think I see Pauline out in the hall,' said Sir. 'In the P.T. class. Yes? Let's have her in.'

Pauline was very small and very frightened. Sir sat her on his knee and told her not to worry. 'All we want to know,' he said, 'is what you said to Tim yesterday. About Sue Nixon and the dead dog.'

'Red sock, Sir,' said Tim.

'Sorry. Red sock. Well, Pauline?'

Pauline looked as if she might join Ruth in tears. Ruth had just realized that she was no longer involved, and was crying with relief.

'You said Miss Middleton gave you a message for Sue Nixon. What was it?'

'It wasn't Sue Nixon,' said Pauline, damply. 'It was June Nichols. It wasn't Miss Middleton, it was Miss Wimbledon.'

'There is no Miss Wimbledon,' said Sir. 'June

Nichols, yes. I know June, but Miss Wimbledon. . . ?'

'She means Miss Wimpole, Sir,' said Tim. 'The big girls call her Wimbledon 'cause she plays tennis, Sir, in a little skirt.'

'I thought you didn't know any girls,' said Sir. 'What did Miss Wimpole say to you, Pauline?'

'She didn't,' said Pauline. 'It was Moira Thatcher. She said to tell June Nichols to come and see Miss Whatsit before assembly and bring her bed socks.'

'Then why tell Tim?'

'I couldn't find June. June's in his class.'

'I begin to see daylight,' said Sir. 'Not much, but it's there. All right, Pauline. Go and get Moira, please.'

Moira had recently had a new brace fitted across her front teeth. It caught the light when she opened her mouth.

'Yeth, Thir?'

'Moira, take it slowly, and tell us what the message was about June Nichols.'

Moira took a deep breath and polished the brace with her tongue.

'Well, Thir, Mith Wimpole thaid to thell June to thee her before athembly with her wed fw – thw – thth –'

'Frock?' said Sir. Moira nodded gratefully. 'So why tell Pauline?'

'Pauline liveth up her thtweet, Thir.'

'No I don't,' said Pauline. 'They moved. They got a council house, up the Ridgeway.'

'All right, Moira,' said Sir. 'Just ask Miss Wimpole if she could thp – spare me a minute of her time, please?'

If Miss Wimpole was surprised to find eight people in Sir's office, she didn't show it. As there was no longer room to get inside, she stood at the doorway and waved. Sir waved back. Mike instantly decided that Sir fancied Miss Wimpole.

'Miss Wimpole, I believe you must be the last link in the chain. Am I right in thinking that you wanted June Nichols to see you before assembly, with her red frock?'

'Why, yes,' said Miss Wimpole. 'She's dancing a solo at the end-of-term concert. I wanted her to practise, but she didn't turn up.'

'Thank you,' said Sir. 'One day, when we both have a spare hour or two, I'll tell you why she didn't turn up. As for you lot,' he said, turning to the mob round his desk, 'you seem to have been playing Chinese Whispers without knowing it. You also seem to think that the entire staff is off its head. You may be right. I don't know. Red socks, dead dogs, live frogs – we'll put your friend in the school pond, Ruth. Fetch him at break. And now, someone had better find June Nichols and deliver Miss Wimpole's message.'

'Oh, there's no point, Sir. She couldn't have come anyway,' said Ruth. 'She's got chicken-pox. She hasn't been at school for ages.'

Jan Mark

Write

Imagine that a producer decides to make a children's TV play out of this story. Try drawing the main characters: in words. Think not only about how they look, but how they talk and move. Note any eccentric habits.
▶ Mike
▶ Ruth
▶ the Head
▶ Miss Middleton.

Improvise

Like any writer Jan Mark leaves out scenes, allowing the readers to fill them in using their imagination. Try improvising the following scenes using what you have found out about the characters they involve.

Scene 1 Miss Middleton tells the Head what has happened during her lesson. Use these questions to help you get into your parts:

Miss Middleton
▶ How do you get on with Ruth normally?
▶ How did you feel when the frog leapt out?
▶ What do you want the Head to do?
▶ What do you think the pupils feel towards you?
▶ Are your classes normally well-behaved?

The Head
▶ What sort of teacher do you think Miss Middleton is?
▶ What do you normally do in situations like this when pupils appear to be playing practical jokes on teachers?
▶ What do you know about Ruth and Mike? Will that influence your attitude towards Miss Middleton's story?
▶ What sorts of things will you want to ask Miss Middleton when she tells you her version of the story?

Scene 2 What do you think Ruth and Mike said to each other when they got outside the Head's room after the truth had been discovered?

Use these questions to help you get into your parts:

Mike
▶ How did you feel when the Head sent for you?
▶ Do you think Ruth should have involved you?
▶ What was it like when you entered the Head's room?
▶ How did you feel when the truth came out?
▶ What did you notice Ruth doing all through the Head's investigations?
▶ What do you think about the Head, Miss Middleton, Miss Wimpole?

Ruth
▶ How do you feel about Mike after this situation?
▶ Do you blame him for what happened or do you find the whole thing funny?

▶ What did you feel like when the frog jumped onto Miss Middleton?
▶ What was it like for you when the Head was trying to find out about the truth of the situation?
▶ How did you feel when the truth came out?
▶ What do you think about Miss Middleton? What do you think about the way she reacted to the situation?

Write

Now use the ideas you have based your improvisations on to write either Miss Middleton's diary or Ruth's diary.

Remember that diaries are not just records of daily events, they are places to record secret thoughts and feelings.

Miss Middleton, for example, might not only talk about what happened that day but also about:
▶ How she feels about the pupils in her classes, particularly Ruth.
▶ How the Head handled the situation.

If you choose to write Ruth's diary you might like to split it into two entries:

Entry 1 Written on the evening she is told by Mike that she has to bring the dead frog to school.
Entry 2 Written on the evening after the scene with the Head.

③ Reading stories 2

Getting inside the character's head

So far we have suggested that getting to know characters in stories is a bit like getting to know people in real life. Like detectives, we gather clues from all of the above sources and we piece the evidence together and make our judgements about them.

However, it is probably true to say that in most stories we come to know the characters better than we ever get to know people in real life – even those people who are closest to us – because writers can take us inside characters and show us what they are really thinking and feeling.

Betsy Byars is particularly skilful in the way she takes us inside her characters and shows us how they are feeling and what they are thinking.

▶ Read

First let us look at how Mouse handles the situation in Betsy Byars' *Eighteenth Emergency*.

Marv Hammerman has been terrorising Mouse since he caught Mouse writing his name on a poster depicting Neanderthal Man.

▶ HOW DO WRITERS LET US KNOW WHAT IT'S LIKE TO BE SOMEONE ELSE?

Mouse glanced at his watch. It was 9.31. Slowly he walked the half block to Stumpy's, which was a pizza place that had pinball machines. The entrance was below street level, and Mouse stopped and looked inside for a moment. He couldn't see anything at first because his eyes were still accustomed to the bright light outside, but he could hear the sharp mechanical sounds of the pinball machines, the bells, the clicks, the machine-gun bursts of points being scored. He went down the steps.

'Is Marv Hammerman here?' he asked, squinting up at the man behind the counter. The man was putting packs of gum in a display stand. He glanced at Mouse and kept on straightening the gum.

'No, he hasn't been in. Hey, Steve, where's Hammerman?'

The man and Mouse waited while Steve's ball travelled down through the bright maze of the pinball machine. Steve urged the ball into the holes with gentle leaning movements of his body. When it was over he said, 'He may be in later.'

'He may be in later,' the man told Mouse.

'Thanks.' Mouse turned and walked out of Stumpy's. He lifted the cuff of his jacket and checked his watch again. It was 9.36. Slowly he began to walk up the sidewalk. This was the one thing he hadn't thought of – that he wouldn't be able to find Hammerman. He walked two more blocks, turned around and came up the other side of the street.

He thought he would not be able to bear the tension if Hammerman did not appear soon. He crossed in front of Stumpy's and started down the street again, moving a little faster. He thought he had been walking for hours. Where could Hammerman be? He looked at his watch again. It was 9.55.

The sunlight seemed blinding now, and Mouse wanted to dim it so that whatever was going to happen would not be lit up for everyone to see. He walked to the end of the block and squinted down at his watch. It was 9.57. He paused in front of the barber shop to wind his watch and found that it was already wound tightly. He could not remember winding it, but it was that strange kind of day when watches could wind themselves and a minute could become an hour and the sun could shine on one single person like a spotlight.

He started walking. He walked in the same quick way, and he was almost back to the old Rialto theatre when he saw Marv Hammerman coming towards him. Hammerman was with the boy in the black sweat shirt, and both of them were walking quickly as if they had heard Mouse was waiting. The boy in the black sweat shirt was smiling a little.

When Mouse saw them, his walking suddenly became harder. His shoes seemed to stick to the sidewalk, and his legs got heavy. He felt as if he were walking under water. He pulled down his jacket, smoothed his hair, hitched up his pants, kept his hands busy in order to keep attention from his slow heavy feet. He pulled at his ear lobe, wiped his nose, zipped his jacket higher. Foolishly he thought of the hundred and eighteen little people of his father's dreams. He wished they would appear, lift him and carry him away. 'So long, Hammerman,' he would cry as they hurried him to safety.

Mouse kept walking, and the three of them met in front of the Rialto by the boarded-up booth where Mouse used to buy tickets to the Saturday science-fiction specials.

Mouse finished working the zipper on his jacket and pulled his cuffs down. He said to Hammerman, 'I was sick yesterday and I had to go home, but I'm here now.'

It came out in a rush. Mouse hoped that he hadn't said it so quickly that Hammerman didn't hear it. It was important that this one thing be said while he was still able to talk.

'He still looks a little sick to me, don't he to you?' the boy in the black sweat shirt said, smiling. 'Course he looks better than he's *gonna* look.'

Mouse didn't say anything. He was trying to steel himself for the battle. The only thing he knew about fighting, he realized now, was that if you put your thumbs inside your fists and hit somebody hard with your hand like that, you could break your thumb. He rearranged his hands which he had instinctively folded with the thumbs inside.

He cleared his throat, wondering if he was supposed to say something else. He had had so little experience in fighting that he did not know how a fight of this kind, an arranged fight, would actually start. He remembered seeing a fist fight in an old silent movie on television one time, and the opponents had lifted their fists at the same moment, in the same position, and had circled each other in a set pattern. Still he couldn't imagine this fight starting, not in that way or any other. He could only imagine the ending.

The boy in the black sweat shirt jerked his head at Hammerman. He said to Mouse, 'He don't like anybody writing things about him.'

Mouse was so nervous he thought perhaps the boy had been talking to him for hours. He wasn't certain of anything. He said quickly, 'I know.'

The boy in the black sweat shirt nodded at Hammerman again. He said, 'He wants you to know real good.'

The sun went behind a cloud, and it was suddenly dim beneath the marquee. Mouse couldn't see for a minute. He had been looking at the boy in the sweat shirt while he was talking, and now the boy was silent. All Mouse could see was the whiteness of his smile.

Mouse looked back at Hammerman. For a moment he couldn't see him clearly either. Hammerman's face was a pale circle in the darkness, like the children's faces in the hospital ward, lit up by the light from Mouse's flashlight. Then, abruptly, everything snapped into focus. Hammerman's face was so clear there seemed to be nothing between Mouse and Hammerman, not even air. They could have been up in that high altitude area where the air thins and even distant points come into focus.

Hammerman hadn't made a move that Mouse could see. He was still standing with his hands at his sides, his feet apart. But his body had lost its relaxed look and was ready in a way that Mouse's body would never be.

Mouse raised his fists. His thumbs were carefully outside, pointing upward so that he appeared to be handling invisible controls of some sort. Then he saw Hammerman's fist coming towards him, the knuckles like pale pecans, and at the same time Mouse saw Hammerman's eyes, pale also but very bright. Then Hammerman's fist slammed into his stomach.

Mouse doubled over and staggered backwards a few steps. He thought for a moment that he was going to fall to the ground, just sit down like a baby who has lost his balance. He didn't, and after a second he straightened and came towards Hammerman. He threw out his right hand.

He didn't see Hammerman's fist this time, just felt it in the stomach again. It was so hard that Mouse made a strangled noise. If he had eaten breakfast, there would have been Sugar Pops all over the sidewalk from that blow.

From *Eighteenth Emergency*, Betsy Byars

In this passage Betsy Byars tries to show us what it feels like when the victim tries to confront the bully.

Work your way through the extract that you have just read and highlight or make a note of any clues which show strongly how Mouse feels at this point in the story.

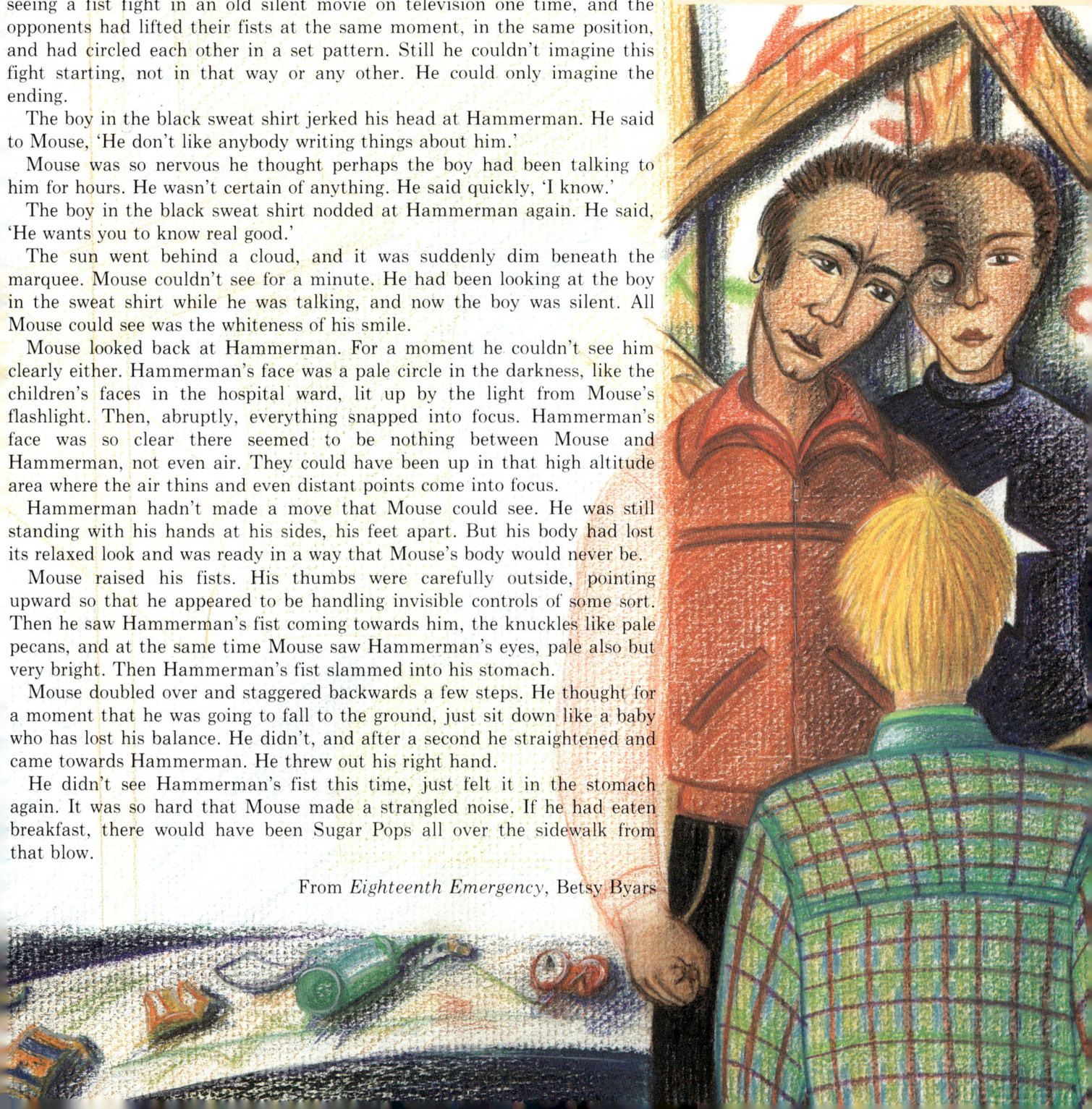

Now compare your work with a partner's.

▶ Have you picked up the same clues?
▶ Which words, phrases or sentences bring out Mouse's feelings most strongly?
▶ Do any of the clues you have found show that Mouse's feelings change in this passage?
▶ Try to work out how the writer has made us share Mouse's feelings at this point.

4 Reading stories 3

Characters: Types or individuals?

Many of the characters you meet in the novels you read will be boys and girls of your own age. When we are reading we often think about how we would react in a similar situation to the one the character finds him or herself in.

Reflect

On p. 93 are two sets of book jackets. Each set pictures artists' impressions of the boy and girl characters contained within the books the covers are promoting.

The artists and the writers seem to have an impression of what boys and girls of your age should be like. What do you think that impression is?

Look at each set carefully. Then copy this grid and fill it in for each set of cover illustrations. Use the illustrations as a starting point for fleshing out the pictures of boys and girls each set of artists and novelists have in mind.

	SET A		SET B	
	BOYS	GIRLS	BOYS	GIRLS
HOBBIES / PASTIMES				
DRESS				
FAVOURITE SUBJECTS AT SCHOOL				
STRONGEST SUBJECTS AT SCHOOL				
FAVOURITE TV PROGRAMMES				
ATTITUDE TOWARDS OPPOSITE SEX				
AMBITIONS				

Set A

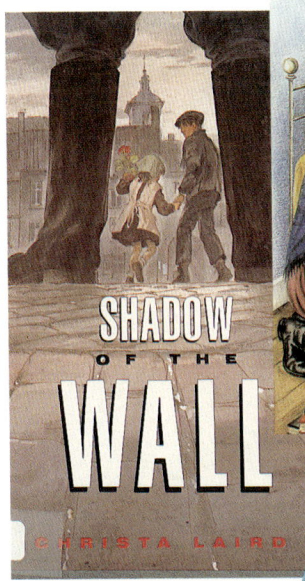

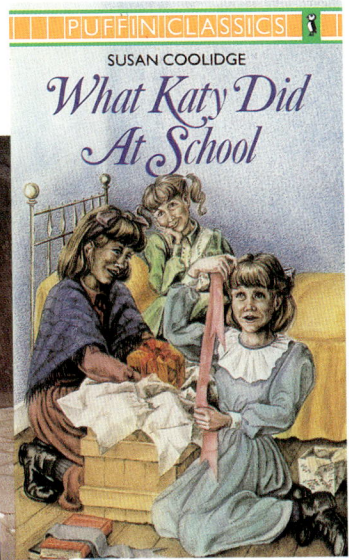

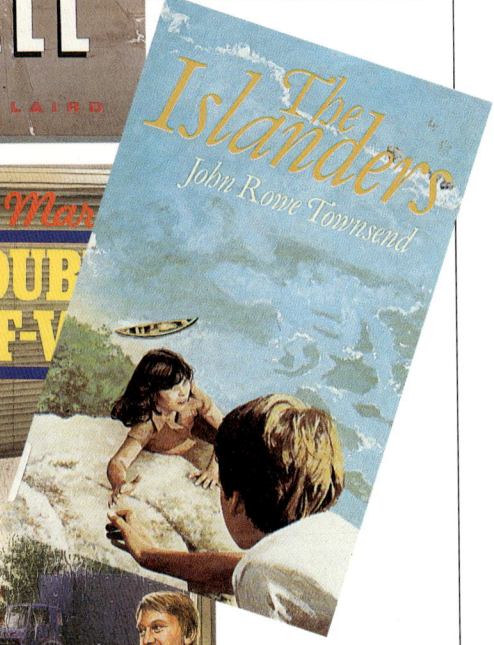

Set B

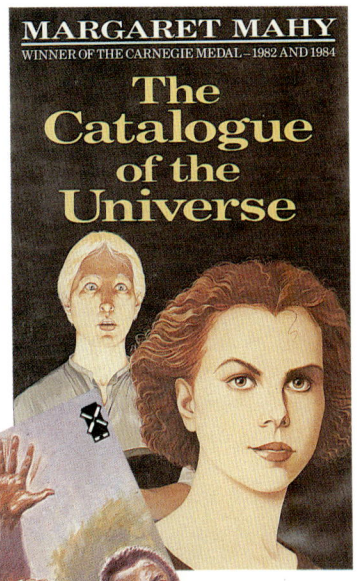

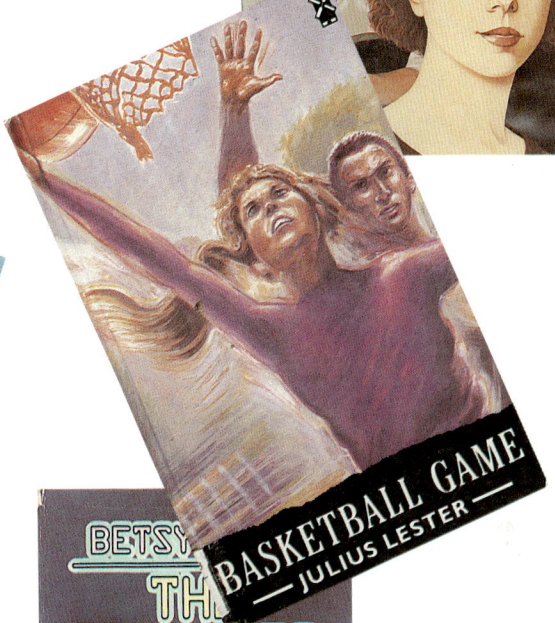

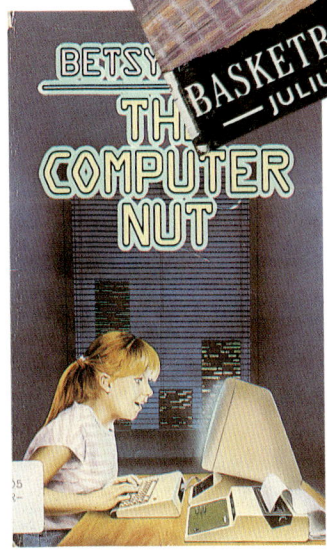

Discuss

Now compare your work with your partner's. Are there any similarities or differences?

Which set of artists' illustrations does your picture of what teenage boys and girls should be like resemble?

Do you resemble any of the people in the pictures? If so, which one?

Where do you think you have got your ideas from about what boys and girls should be like?

ARE THE CHARACTERS WE MEET IN BOOKS DIFFERENT? LIKE US? OR ARE THEY TELLING US WHAT WE SHOULD BE LIKE?

Read and reflect

Read the story of 'Becky and the Wheels-and-brake Boys' carefully.

Becky and the Wheels-and-brake Boys

Even my own cousin Ben was there – riding away, in the ringing of bicycle bells down the road. Every time I came to watch them – see them riding round and round enjoying themselves – they scooted off like crazy on their bikes.

They can't keep doing that. They'll see!

I only want to be with Nat, Aldo, Jimmy and Ben. It's no fair reason they don't want to be with me. Anybody could go off their head for that. Anybody! A girl can not, not, let boys get away with it all the time.

Bother! I have to walk back home, alone.

I know total-total that if I had my own bike, the Wheels-and-brake Boys wouldn't treat me like that. I'd just ride away with them, wouldn't I?

Over and over I told my mum I wanted a bike. Over and over she looked at me as if I was crazy. 'Becky, d'you think you're a boy? Eh? D'you think you're a boy? In any case, where's the money to come from? Eh?'

Of course I know I'm not a boy. Of course I know I'm not crazy. Of course I know all that's no reason why I can't have a bike. No reason! As soon as I get indoors I'll just have to ask again – ask Mum once more.

At home, indoors, I didn't ask my mum.

I was allowed no chance whatsoever. No chance to talk to Mum about the bike I dream of day and night! And I knew exactly the bike I wanted. I wanted a bike like Ben's bike. Oh, I wished I still had even my scorpion on a string to run up and down somebody's back!

I answered my mum. 'Yes, mam.' I went off into Meg's and my bedroom.

I sat down at the little table, as well I might. Could homework stay in anybody's head in broad daylight outside? No. Could I keep a bike like Ben's out of my head? Not one bit. That bike took me all over the place. My beautiful bike jumped every log, every rock, every fence. My beautiful bike did everything cleverer than a clever cowboy's horse, with me in the saddle. And the bell, the bell was such a glorious gong of a ring!

If Dad was alive I could talk to him. If Dad was alive he'd give me money for the bike like a shot.

After dinner, I combed my hair in the bedroom. Mum did her machining on the verandah. Meggie helped Mum. Granny sat there, wishing she could take on any job, as usual.

I told Mum I was going to make up a quarrel with Shirnette. I went, but my friend wouldn't speak to me, let alone come out to keep my company. I stood alone and watched the Wheels-and-brake Boys again.

This time the boys didn't race away past me. I stood leaning against the tall coconut palm tree. People passed up and down. The nearby main road was busy with traffic. But I didn't mind. I watched the boys. Riding round and round the big Flame-tree, Nat, Aldo, Jimmy and Ben looked marvellous.

At first each boy rode round the tree alone. Then each boy raced each other round the tree, going round three times. As he won, the winner rang his bell on and on, till he stopped panting and could laugh and talk properly. Next, most reckless and fierce, all the boys raced against each other. And, leaning against their bicycles, talking and joking, the boys popped soft drinks open, drank and ate chipped bananas.

I walked up to Nat, Aldo, Jimmy and Ben and said, 'Can somebody teach me to ride?'

'Why don't you stay indoors and learn to cook and sew and wash clothes?' Jimmy said.

I grinned. 'I know all that already,' I said. 'And one day perhaps I'll even be mum to a boy child, like all of you. Can you cook and sew and wash clothes, Jimmy? All I want is to learn to ride. I want you to teach me.'

I didn't know why I said what I said. But everybody went silent and serious.

One after the other, Nat, Aldo, Jimmy and Ben got on to their bikes and rode off. I wasn't at all cross with them. I only wanted to be riding out of the playground with them. I knew they'd be heading into the town to have ice-cream and things and talk and laugh.

Mum was sitting alone on the verandah. She sewed buttons on to a white shirt she'd made. I sat down next to Mum. Straightaway, 'Mum,' I said, 'I still want to have a bike badly.'

'Oh, Becky, you still have that foolishness in your head? What am I going to do?'

Mum talked with some sympathy. Mum knew I was honest. 'I can't get rid of it, mam,' I said.

Mum stopped sewing. 'Becky,' she said, staring in my face, 'how many girls around here do you see with bicycles?'

'Janice Gordon has a bike,' I reminded her.

'Janice Gordon's dad has acres and acres of coconuts and bananas, with a business in the town as well.'

I knew Mum was just about to give in. Then my granny had to come out on to the verandah and interfere. Listen to that Granny-Liz. 'Becky, I heard your mother tell you over and over she can't afford to buy you a bike. Yet you keep on and on. Child, you're a girl.'

'But I don't want a bike because I'm a girl.'

'D'you want it because you feel like a boy?' Granny said.

'No. I only want a bike because I want it and want it and want it.'

Granny just carried on. 'A tomboy's like a whistling woman and a crowing hen, who can only come to a bad end. D'you understand?'

I didn't want to understand. I knew Granny's speech was an awful speech. I went and sat down with Lenny and Vin, who were making a kite.

By Saturday morning I felt real sorry for Mum. I could see Mum really had it hard for money. I had to try and help. I knew anything of Dad's – anything – would be worth a great mighty hundred pounds.

I found myself in the centre of town, going through the busy Saturday crowd. I hoped Mum wouldn't be too cross. I went into the fire station. With lots of luck I came face to face with a round face man in uniform. He talked to me. 'Little miss, can I help you?'

I told him I'd like to talk to the head man. He took me into the office and gave me a chair. I sat down. I opened out my brown paper parcel. I showed him my dad's sun helmet. I told him I thought it would make a good fireman's hat. I wanted to sell the helmet for some money towards a bike, I told him.

The fireman laughed a lot. I began to laugh too. The fireman put me in a car and drove me back home.

Mum's eyes popped to see me bringing home the fireman. The round face fireman laughed at my adventure. Mum laughed too, which was really good. The fireman gave Mum my dad's hat back. Then, mystery, mystery, Mum sent me outside while they talked.

My mum was only a little cross with me. Then – mystery and more mystery – my mum took me with the fireman in his car to his house.

The fireman brought out what? A bicycle! A beautiful, shining bicycle! His nephew's bike. His nephew had been taken away, all the way to America. The bike had been left with the fireman-uncle for him to sell it. And the good kind fireman-uncle decided we could have the bike – on small payments. My mum looked uncertain. But, in a big, big way the fireman knew it was all right. And mum smiled a little. My mum had good sense to know it was all right. My mum took the bike from the fireman Mister Dean.

And guess what? Seeing my bike much, much newer than his, my cousin Ben's eyes popped with envy. But – he took on the big job. He taught me to ride. Then he taught Shirnette.

I ride into town with the Wheels-and-brake Boys now. When she can borrow a bike, Shirnette comes too. We all sit together. We have patties and ice-cream and drink drinks together. We talk and joke. We ride about, all over the place.

And, again, guess what? Fireman Mister Dean became our best friend, and Mum's especially. He started coming round almost everyday.

James Berry

Now look at these artist's impressions of the main character. Which do you think comes closest to your mental impression of the main character?

Be very clear in your minds about why the picture you select matches the character in the story.

Discuss

Now compare your picture selection with your partner's and compare your reasons for your decision. Which of you can produce the strongest argument to support your choice? Did you agree? Did your partner think of reasons for his/her choice that you did not think of?

When you have finished look at the following pupils' reactions to this story. Discuss whether you think they are right or not? Be careful to justify your opinion.

"The problem with Becky's mum is that she thinks all girls are delicate and weak, but they're not, you know, or at least they don't have to be."

"Becky thinks that boys have all the fun: that's right. Parents always stop their daughters from doing the exciting things that they let their sons do."

"The mum's real reason for stopping Becky from having a bike is that the family can't afford it. No-one can really believe that girls shouldn't have bikes."

"This story is set in the West Indies: girls are treated differently in Britain."

"I think the message of this story is that girls should have the same chances as boys."

Write

Did you find this story surprising? Or did you find Becky's behaviour fairly typical? This unit has attempted to show that some people have stereotype views of what boys and girls should be like. Do you?

Try writing your own story in which a boy or girl character does not conform to these stereotype views of boys and girls.

5 People in poems

Getting inside a poem

As a reader, you do not just meet characters through stories. Poems too show us what it is like to be other people. Because poems use fewer words than stories, we have to be particularly careful about picking up all the clues the poet supplies in his poem. We cannot afford to miss any!

Read and discuss

Here is a poem, written by a school boy, Danny Cerqueira. He has written on a subject about which he feels very strongly. Not only do we learn something about what he is describing, but we also learn something about Danny himself.

We have not printed the title of this poem to help you focus on the clues in the lines, which you have to pick up if you are going to work out what this poem is about. This will not be easy, but poems are not always easy to read. Later on in this course you will find out why. For the moment, stick at the task and you will be surprised at what you can find in the poem.

One of the group should read the poem aloud.

> Walking
> with mother,
> Like it always does,
> Wading through the rainy weather
> It always looks for us.
>
> Running
> Towards us,
> Hoping to play,
> hands wagging lifelessly,
> A sign to run away.
>
> Staring
> From the steamed up window.
> "Is HE looking at us?"
> Eyes that never meet eyes,
> Looking from the bus.
>
> Danny Cerqueira

When you have heard the poem read out loud, first try to agree on an appropriate title for the poem.

Then take it in turns to ask the rest of the group questions about parts of the poem you don't understand.

When you are listening to the other group members' questions, try to suggest answers, pointing to words and phrases in the poem to support your ideas. It does not matter if you are wrong. Just say what you think. It will give your group something to work on.

When you have listened to all your group's questions and worked out what you can about the poem, one of the group should present your ideas about the poem to the class. Ask the class as a whole the questions about the poem which you still have not answered. Someone in the class might be able to shed light on your difficulties and give you an idea to start working on.

Now read Danny's explanation of his poem. You will notice that he discusses how he tried to get his ideas and feelings across in his poem, 'Mentally Handicapped'.

It was an extra hot day and no-one wanted to do any work, let alone write poetry, the most dreaded English topic. However it was impossible to get out of it. As it was the International Year of the Disabled the poems were to be on the theme of the disabled. At first, like everyone else in the class I was very reluctant to do it but as I said there was no getting out of it. I tried to go about it in a methodical way and thought carefully about what to write.

The whole poem was taken from memories of when I was about nine years old. A mongol boy lived across the road from me. I never used to play with him because he was different and I was afraid of that. Whenever he saw me he'd shout out, 'What's your name, boy?' Although I always used to tell him, he'd ask me the same question the next time he saw me. I now realise that his mother must have been the most patient of people. I dedicated the first verse to her because she devoted herself to him and even walked out in the rain with him to keep him happy. His mother was the one I always saw him with and she was his best friend.

While thinking of that boy (I never learnt his name) I remembered a mentally handicapped girl. Although I never saw her as often as the boy I did learn her name. Her name was Naomi and about six years ago she was twenty two years old and very much dependent on her mother. The second verse is dedicated to Naomi.

It was one day in particular which inspired me to write the second verse. I was with a couple of friends and we were waiting for their mother. We were laughing and having fun when Naomi saw us. Obviously she wanted to join in the fun and ran ahead of her mother towards us. Her hands wagged when she ran. We heard a voice, 'Quick, get away from there.' I was ready to run before I heard the voice and ran across the road rapidly without thinking about cars. My friends and I took the incident with nervous excitement. I felt terribly guilty afterwards but I didn't tell anyone of my guilt lest my friends laughed at me. This brings me to the shape of the poem. I isolated the words at the beginning of each verse to show that

FIND YOUR WAY THROUGH POEMS.

mentally handicapped people do like to do what any other person does. I write the HE in the third verse in block capitals to show that mentally handicapped people have their own personalities. They are a he or a she not an IT. Many people exaggerate greatly when they pretend not to know whether a mongol is a boy or a girl. I made the other lines shorter to make the poem look more interesting.

Finally the last verse was again referring to a particular day: while I was waiting for the bus to go to school, the familiar blue bus stopped in the traffic. The other people at the bus stop pretended not to see the children lolling up and down in the bus. I saw the boy of whom I write inside. His dull eyes were staring out of his hanging head. He was breathing onto the window so that it steamed up and hid his face. That memory was the first thing I remembered when writing the poem and I doubt that it is one that I shall ever forget.

How many of the clues that Danny mentions did you pick up? It doesn't matter if you missed them, hopefully you are beginning to learn what to look for in poems.

Read and reflect

Here is another poem about a different person. Read it carefully:

Winter Days

On winter mornings in the playground
The boys stand huddled,
Their cold hands doubled
Into trouser pockets.
The air **hangs** frozen
About the buildings
And the cold is an ache in the blood
And a pain on the tender skin
Beneath finger nails.
The odd shouts
Sound off **like struck iron**
And the sun
Balances white
Above the boundary wall.
I fumble my bus ticket
Between numb fingers
Into a fag,
Take a drag
And blow white smoke
Into the December air.

Gareth Owen

Jot down any impressions you have about the person in this poem.

Now let us see where your impressions came from. Work your way through the poem looking for patterns in the words. What we mean by 'patterns' is any similarities, repetitions or contrasts in the words the poet has used.

Now let us have a look at the images, Gareth Owen has used.

LANGUAGE NOTE

Images are frequently used by writers of poetry and stories to help us picture in our minds what the writer is describing.

All images are based on comparisons and usually let us see what the writer is describing in a new way. For example, the image 'the teacher had a nose like a conker' not only conjures up a picture of the appearance of the teacher's round, shiny nose, it also makes him appear rather silly.

The images in 'Winter Days' have been picked out for you in bold print. If we try rewriting these images in plain English, we get something like

The air hangs frozen	**It was a bit foggy**
The odd shouts **Sound off like struck iron**	**You could hear loud shouts**
the sun Balances white **Above the boundary wall**	**The sun rises above the** **boundary wall**

Look at the rewrites carefully. Why do you think the poet used images and not plain English in the way that we have? It would certainly have made the poem easier to understand. Has the poem lost anything, if you substitute the plain English rewrites for images?

Discussion

Now try sharing your ideas with your partner about this poem and about how the writer has got his ideas across. You could use these questions to help you:

▶ How do the boys in the poem feel?
▶ What mental picture do you have of the scene the poet describes?
▶ How does the poet feel towards the boys he describes?
▶ How does the poet get across the idea of coldness?

6 Reading for information 1

Finding facts

We found in Module 2: Reading that we do not always read for the same reason every time we read. We often read texts at school to find information. Though you may not have thought about it, this means you have to read them in an entirely different way. This exercise will help you discover how we can do this.

Research

Carry out your own research into the way people read.

You will need: one stop watch, two readers, two observer/timers and the passage from 'Choosing a bicycle'.

Instructions:
This experiment involves the readers in a race against time. They must extract the information requested at the end of the passage as quickly as possible. Each answer must be found separately – one round per question.

a) The readers should start with the passage face down on the desk.

b) On the word 'Go' the readers should attempt to be first to find the answer to the first question.

c) As soon as one reader has found the information to the question, the other reader must stop and the round comes to an end. The observers should check the answer, record the time the successful reader took to answer the question and award one mark for

TWO WAYS HOW TO FIND INFORMATION QUICKLY.

each correct, first answer. If the answer is incorrect the round must start again.

d) Repeat this process for each question. The winner is the reader with the most marks.

e) Whilst readers are looking for the answers to the questions, the observers should watch each reader carefully and note down anything the reader is doing which seems to be helping him/her find the correct answer. (*Hint*: Watch their eyes carefully and see if they do anything with their hands to help them.)

Choosing a bicycle

With so much choice on the market today, how do you know which bicycle is right for you? Start by thinking carefully about your needs, now and in the future, and your budget. Do you want it for town use, or perhaps riding in the country? Do you want something which will take some hard use, for off-road riding, or lightweight cycletouring? Where and how are you going to store it when not in use?

If possible, read one of the guides to buying a cycle currently available. Try to become familiar with some of the terminology. Buy from a reputable dealer who will offer advice when you are looking and a maintenance service after you purchase a cycle. Women should not let themselves be fobbed off with the chauvinist view that 'A small-wheeled shopper is all you need' – unless that is truly the case. Racing bikes and touring bikes may look the same to the untrained eye, but they handle quite differently on the road. If you want more information than your local shop can provide – or simply an independent opinion – contact your local cycling club.

Type of bike
SMALL-WHEELED BIKES OR SHOPPERS
Fine for children who are too small for large-wheeled models, and adults who are going only as far as the local shops and aren't carrying large loads. Where storage or carriage of the machine is a problem, folding models are a solution, but, other than the most expensive designs, they give a generally inferior ride to rigid-frame bicycles.

COMMUTER BIKES OR TOWN BIKES
Although these may look the same as touring or racing bikes, a cycle particularly suited to commuting will usually need only 3 or 5 gears (unless you live in a hilly area) which could be built into the hub rather than involving a derailleur shifting mechanism. A softer saddle and wider tyres will make pot-holes a bit easier to take, though they will slow you down. Straighter front forks than normally found on a touring cycle will give better steering control in traffic. Partial toe clips are useful for positioning your feet correctly on the pedals, and fittings for lights are essential.

TOURING BIKES
Equipped with full-sized wheels, upright or dropped handlebars, 5 or more gears and carrier racks, these are more comfortable to ride over long distances and are generally preferred by many adult cyclists. The gears should offer a wide range of ratios (from the low or mid-30''s to around 90''), the saddle should be firm, with perhaps a little padding (NOT soft or sprung), toe clips and straps should be fitted (whether or not you tighten them up), and the lighter the whole machine is the easier it will be to ride.

RACING BIKES

Designed for speed rather than comfort, stripped of mudguards, carrier racks and lights, and fitted with narrow tyres and fairly straight forks, these machines are great for racing but a poor choice for general use. If you are considering taking up cycle racing, you might seek the guidance and opinions of members of a racing club or specialist cycle shop before making an expensive purchase.

OTHER TYPES

Tandems, tricycles, mountain bikes and BMX cycles provide unique riding experiences. National clubs and local groups particular to each type of machine have been set up and will happily give advice on purchases, technical information, riding techniques etc.

Size

It is important to get the right size of bike if you want to be comfortable and feel in control, particularly if you are planning to do any touring. In general you need to be able to straddle the frame (if the bike has a cross-bar) with both feet flat on the ground, and when sitting on the saddle, be just able to put one foot down. In more technical terms, for standard design bicycles the length of the frame tube which extends down from the saddle to the bottom bracket should be about 9–10" shorter than your inside leg length (shoes off). The saddle can be raised a couple of inches above the frame, but if that still isn't enough you may need a larger frame. The saddle is at the correct height when you can put your heels on the pedals and feel that your legs are pretty straight.

The distance from the nose of the saddle to the handlebars is also important. Putting your elbow against the saddle, you should just reach the top of the bars. Saddles can be adjusted a small amount forward or back, and different length handlebar stems are available to help get this right. Many cyclists' complaints of back or neck ache are due to being cramped or o-v-e-r-s-t-r-e-t-c-h-e-d.

Questions

1 Which paragraph makes reference to '3–5 gears'?
2 Which paragraph mentions BMX bikes?
3 Which paragraph deals with the problems of overstretching?
4 Which paragraph deals with the problems of pot-holes?
5 What does the writer mean by a 'wide range of ratios' when referring to gears?
6 Why are partial toe clips helpful for cyclists?
7 Where might you find advice on buying bicycles?
8 Which type of bike is best for long distance cycling?
9 Why is finding the right size of bike important?
10 How do you know when the bike is the right size?

Discuss

Now you need to discover the reasons for the winner's success. Take it in turns to explain what went on in the experiment.

a) The winner should explain how he or she went about finding the answers to each question. Was his/her technique always the same? Did he or she have to vary it, according to the type of question?
b) The loser should explain the technique he or she adopted. Was it different to the winner's?
c) The observers should describe what they saw during the experiment.

Once you have listened to each other's account of what happened, try and describe a method for quickly

a) finding paragraphs/lines where you might find information on the subject you're looking for (e.g. questions 1–4).

b) finding specific facts (e.g. questions 5–10).

Now, working together, produce a flow-chart that demonstrates each of these methods.

A really crucial guide to....

Skimming and scanning

There are proper names for the skills the successful reader uses when he or she is looking for information.

Skimming: when you were looking for paragraphs that gave you the information to questions 1–4, you did not need to read the paragraphs in close detail, all you had to do was to read it through quickly to get the gist of it.

Scanning: when you are looking for specific information, again you do not have to read the whole book or page in close detail. It is quicker to fix a key word or phrase in your mind that the author might use when dealing with the subject you are interested in, and just run your eyes over the page until you find him using it. For question 5, for example, you might have scanned the page, looking for the word 'ratios'.

7 Reading for information 2

Finding out facts for yourself

In the last unit you looked at how we select information from a text. In this case the facts were supplied for you.

What happens, however, if you have to find out your facts for yourself? How do you go about it?

This is how Indira went about researching the subject of Diwali, a Hindu New Year festival, so that she could give a talk to her classmates.

Choosing your sources

I thought that my mum and dad could give me some information about Diwali but I did not think they would know much about the history, so I thought I'd go to the library as well.

Knowing your questions

I knew what happens during Diwali in this country, but I wanted to know the answer to these questions: what happens in other countries during Diwali? Is it different or the same? When and why did the festival begin?

Using your sources

a) **Interviews**

I talked to my mum and dad. I asked them questions about Diwali to see if they could tell me anything I didn't know about it. I worked out my questions beforehand. They showed me some photos of Diwali in India and I asked them questions about these photos and noted down their answers.

b) **The library**

I went to the library to see if they had any books on Diwali.

Using the library

Before I could find any books on Diwali I had to settle on some **keywords:** words or phrases in the titles of books that might show that they had the information I was looking for. My words were: Diwali, Religious festivals, Festivals, Celebrations, Hindu, Hinduism.

My school library had a computer catalogue system, so I punched these words in one at a time and copied out the lists that appeared on the screen. I took care to take a note of the **Dewey number** because that showed me where to find the book.

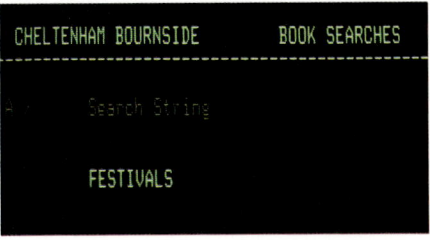

CHELTENHAM BOURNSIDE   BOOK SEARCHES

Search String

FESTIVALS

My local library still has a card catalogue, so I checked what was the Dewey number for books about Eastern religions and looked through the cards with that number for titles of books with my keywords in them.

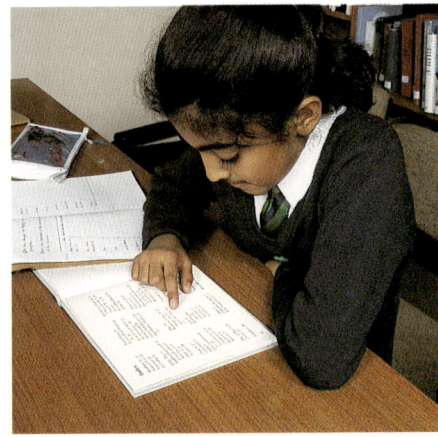

Using the books

When I found a book on the shelves with one of my keywords in it, I first looked at the **contents page**, which had the chapter titles to see if any of them also contained one of my keywords, particularly Diwali.

I also checked the **index** at the back of the book for my keywords.

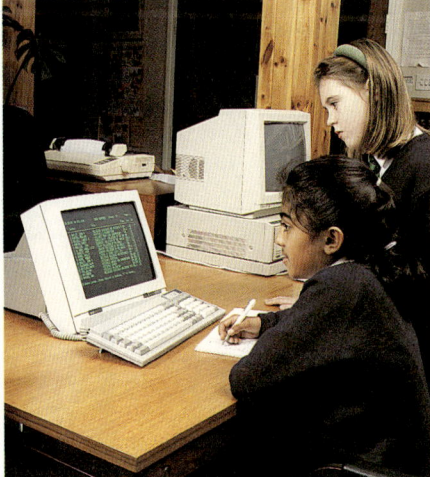

When I found a useful chapter, I scanned each page looking for any **headings** that might suggest they would be helpful. I then scanned the text on each page looking for the word Diwali.

If I found a useful section, I read it carefully with the questions I wanted to answer in mind.

Once I was sure that the page contained information I wanted to use, I tried to jot down in my own words what the book was saying. I split my notes up into sections, using the questions I wanted to answer as headings.

Now try using this process yourself to research a subject that you are really interested in, which you want to talk to a group of your classmates about.

HOW TO MAKE THE LIBRARY WORK FOR YOU.

8 Fact and opinion

Facing the facts

As you found out in Module 2: Reading, not all the reading you do in a day is fiction. Some of your reading deals with facts. But what are facts? Sometimes readers get confused between facts and opinions and this has disastrous results!

To help you learn the difference, here is some more detective work. Below is all the evidence collected by Detective Sergeant Hughes when she visited the scene of the crime at Hinton Hall.

Read and discuss

In a group, solve the crime. There are four suspects:

Lesley Harris
Mrs Jackie Ballinger
Robert Watts
Sir Ian Ballinger

You must discover who committed the crime, the criminal's motive for the crime and when the crime took place. You must also be sure that you can prove your conclusions by collecting evidence. This evidence must consist of provable facts; opinions are no good in a court of law.

CRIME: ROBBERY OF VALUABLES AND CASH WORTH OVER £450,000 FROM THE SAFE OF SIR IAN BALLINGER — OWNER OF HINTON HALL. SAFE IN SIR IAN BALLINGER'S STUDY.

ESTIMATED TIME OF CRIME: BETWEEN 11.05 AND 11.20 A.M.

THE PLAN OF THE HOUSE WHERE THE CRIME TOOK PLACE:

EVIDENCE FOUND AT THE SCENE OF THE CRIME: A PIECE OF CRUMPLED PAPER WITH THE COMBINATION OF THE SAFE WRITTEN UPON IT; A SIZE TEN BOOT PRINT OUTSIDE THE WINDOW OF THE STUDY WHICH HAD BEEN BROKEN; A BROKEN WINDOW PANE WITH PIECES OF BROKEN GLASS LYING IN THE FLOWER BED OUTSIDE; AND A SMASHED FIGURINE LYING ON THE FLOOR NEAR TO THE BROKEN WINDOW OF THE STUDY;

Sergeant Hughes' police notebook

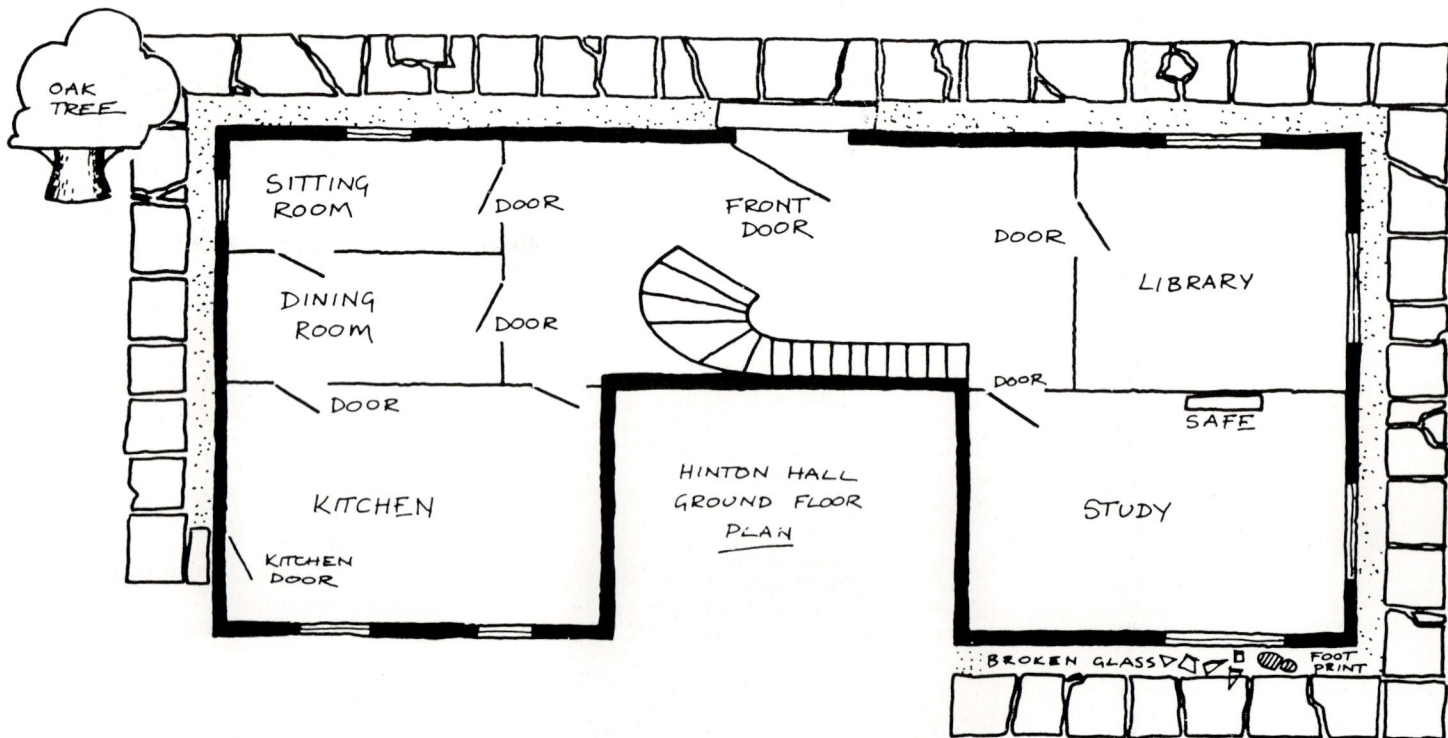

OAK TREE

SITTING ROOM   DOOR   FRONT DOOR   DOOR   LIBRARY

DINING ROOM   DOOR

DOOR   DOOR   SAFE

KITCHEN   HINTON HALL GROUND FLOOR PLAN   STUDY

KITCHEN DOOR

BROKEN GLASS   FOOT PRINT

WHAT IS THE DIFFERENCE BETWEEN A FACT AND AN OPINION?

Robert Watts :

Yes, I'm the village postman. I get to Hinton Hall about 11.00 a.m. most days, but on Monday I was a couple of minutes late. Mrs Jackson, the village postmistress, kept me talking, you see. I only had one letter for Sir Ian. It was a registered letter. He's been having a lot of registered letters lately. They've all got return addresses printed on the back. They're from London mostly, from banks and solicitors. I reckon he's having a spot of money trouble, know what I mean? Anyway, I couldn't get an answer, so I went round the back and had a look through the study window. Sir Ian's a bit deaf and it's a big house, so he doesn't always hear the bell. I often have to knock on his study window to get him or his secretary to answer the door. He wasn't there so I started walking back round to the front, when I bumped into Mrs Ballinger, the old man's daughter-in-law: she was running as if she had the devil behind her. She stopped when she saw me and she looked really guilty, as if I'd caught her up to something. She said something about a dog chasing her and when I explained I couldn't get an answer, she signed for the letter and I went. You know, I didn't see any dog. Sir Ian hates them. The village dogs seem to know that and keep away from the place. I reckon they're frightened he might shoot them given a chance.

Jackie Ballinger:

, I am Sir Ian's daughter-in-law. I live nearby Kensbury and I'd just popped over see if Sir Ian was all right. He's getting absent-minded, you see, and Timothy, my usband, and I are so worried about him, ving all on his own. He doesn't look after mself properly, you know. I arrived at .05 precisely. I know that because I had e radio on in the car when I drove up the ive, and the announcer had just given e time. I must have rung the bell for good 5 minutes, but couldn't get an answer. was obviously very worried. It's so unusual or Sir Ian not to be up and about at that ime. I was just wondering what I should o, when this enormous dog appeared from ehind the oak tree by the corner of the ouse. It was one of those Rottweiler things, think. I am terrified of dogs - you read uch dreadful things in the papers, don't you. I know it was silly but I just took o my heels and ran. I turned the corner at the back of the house and came upon the postman acting very suspiciously. He seemed to be banging at the window, trying to break the glass, I think. I'd obviously caught him in the act of trying to break in. He's your culprit. It's obvious. He has a shifty sort of look and you only have to look at the way he dresses to know he's short of money. I didn't let on I'd seen him. I just signed for Sir Ian's letter and saw him off the premises. He must have come back when the coast was clear. I pushed the letter through the letter box and went off to the nearest phone box to ring my husband and ask what I should do. I returned at about 11.45 to find that there had been a break-in.

Lesley Harris:

Yes, I'm Sir Ian's secretary. I arrived at the Hall at 10.00 as usual, even though it was my last day at work and I certainly didn't feel like going in. I rang the bell and after a little while Sir Ian finally got round to letting me in. At the moment we're engaged in some very important business deals which could make Sir Ian a very rich man. We worked in the study until 11.15. I went to the kitchen to make Sir Ian a coffee, picking up a registered letter which had been pushed through the letter box on my way. Sir Ian went to his library to look for a business directory that we needed to find out some addresses for the letters we had been working on. It took me about ten minutes to make the coffee. Just as I was about to make the coffee, I heard some barking and I looked out of the window to see Sir Ian's daughter-in-law running alongside the building. She's the one you ought to look at carefully, I'm sure she's after Sir Ian's money. I caught her looking in Sir Ian's desk in the study the other day. She knows Sir Ian keeps the combination number to the safe, written on a piece of paper in his desk. I'm sure she was looking for that! I told Sir Ian. He was really angry. She and her husband,Timothy, had asked him for a key about a month ago, just in case of accidents.Sir Ian insisted that she give the key back to him.

Sir Ian Ballinger:

Yes, I'm Sir Ian Ballinger. Mrs Harris arrived at the normal time and we got down to work. You know, these next two weeks could make me a multi-millionaire. She went down to the kitchen to make coffee and I went into the library to look up some addresses. I suppose that must have been about quarter past eleven. I had just started looking for my business directory when I heard some barking which is a bit strange round here, because dogs don't usually venture into this part of the village. Then about five minutes later I heard something smash. At the time I supposed it must have been Mrs Harris dropping something in the kitchen but, come to think of it now, it was probably the window in the study. The noise certainly sounded nearer than the kitchen. Anyway, I found the addresses I wanted and returned to the study to find an empty safe and a smashed window. It was a bit embarrassing. It was Mrs Harris' last day of work for me. I'd given her her notice a month ago. It's a shame really: she lives on her own since her husband died and her little job with me is her only source of income. But I had to let her go: I need someone a bit more up-to-date, who can work a word processor and a fax machine! Her redundancy money was in the safe, and I haven't been able to get to the bank yet to replace it.

Before you turn to the answer on p. 136, check that you have not been led astray by the opinions and the lies that you have met in the statements of the suspects.

Use a grid like this to help you check your facts. Make a copy of the grid and complete it for each suspect:

PROVEN FACTS	OPINIONS	LIES

Now check your proven facts against the evidence at the scene of the crime. Have you changed your mind or are you even more convinced that you have found the culprit?

Turn to p. 136. Were you right? If you were not, try to work out why you went wrong.

What is the difference between a fact and an opinion?

⑨ Project: using your research skills

Travelling through time

Read and reflect

In this module you have had some advice about how you might find information from books in the library. In this unit you will have a chance to use your reading for information skills and your writing skills.

Read the excerpt from Roger Green's *The Devil Finds Work*.

The last her friends saw of Connie was when Paul shouted to her through the snowstorm.

'Connie . . . Hey up, Connie? Connie . . . you're not supposed to go through the Devil's Garden and over the bridge to the village. It's not allowed any more.'

Connie ignored Paul. She walked down the steps to the sunken mysterious garden and into the swirling smoking January snowstorm: a blizzard of snow that became more blinding every minute as though an unseen and devilish hand were controlling the storm.

Connie did not care in the least. She would go through the Devil's Garden, a daft name anyway, she thought, then she would go home to the village over the ancient three-arched bridge: a strange bridge, that had an ugly twisted worn carving of a woman's face on the north side over the middle arch. The villagers had for a long time called it the Witches' Bridge. Once over the bridge she would trudge the two miles through the lonely snow-filled roaring woods to her home in the village. And if it wasn't allowed she did not care. She would do what she wanted for a change.

For Connie was in terrible trouble. She went down the steep curving steps to the sunken garden; the steps were treacherous, half hidden under fan-shaped drifts of snow. Connie nearly fell but saved herself, her cheap black cloak flapping in the rising east wind. The Garden was shrouded in snow and shadow. Her cheap boots were already leaking.

She began to cry. Misery overwhelmed her. She was twelve years old. She had left school at Christmas and had been two weeks in her new job. Now—she had been sacked. Dismissed from her fine new job as under-housemaid at the great Castle that loomed up behind her through the stinging snow. They said at the Castle her bags would follow. They did not want her. Her fine new job working for the rich and mighty at the great Castle was gone. Lost for ever.

And what would she tell mam? Her mam had been so pleased when she heard her Connie had got a secure job as a maid at the Castle. Connie's mother had boasted in the village . . . 'Two o' my lasses are maids up at the Castle, working for Lord Blackdon, you know. My two lasses are a grand help to me, with their dad dead and gone . . .'

Connie wept. Now she had let her mam down. Connie cried bitterly. Everything had gone wrong. She did not care if Paul Bailey, one of the gardener's boys at the Castle, saw her. He was a friend anyway. In fact Paul was in another part of the Castle gardens now, knocking snow off the evergreen trees with a long snow pole.

Paul thought Connie was alone in the Garden. Connie, crying with the thought of telling her mam, thought she was alone, apart from Paul. They were wrong.

Connie wiped her eyes. It was a right creepy place. She wiped her nose on the rough wool of her cloak, wet and cold with shining ice crystals. She hated Lord bloody Blackdon. She hated his Devil's Garden. Hatred made the tears dry. She blinked away the snow. She knew he was always showing his friends the Garden with its ugly collection. He did not seem interested in the world of 1884 with its railways, trams, gaslight and iron. He just wanted to surround himself with old and evil things. Well, she was glad to be going from his horrible Castle and Garden. But not yet, for there was mam to tell . . .

From *The Devil Finds Work*, Roger Green

Copy the grid opposite and list in the left-hand column all the details in this extract that tell you that this story does not take place in the present day. In the right-hand column write down what you think the writer would have written if he'd set the story in the 1990s.

HISTORICAL DETAILS IN THE EXTRACT	MODERN EQUIVALENTS

Discuss

Compare your list with your partner's. When do you think the story is set?

In your grid you have listed individual details taken from the story. Now, with your partner, try and draw up a list of the *types* of detail that Roger Green has used that clearly set the story in the past.

As you can see, writers like Roger Green work very hard to recreate a sense of what it was like to live in the periods they set their stories in. In order to do this they have to spend a lot of time researching life during that period. The pictures below show some possible sources of information about the past that they can use. With your partner work out what sorts of information each of these sources could supply.

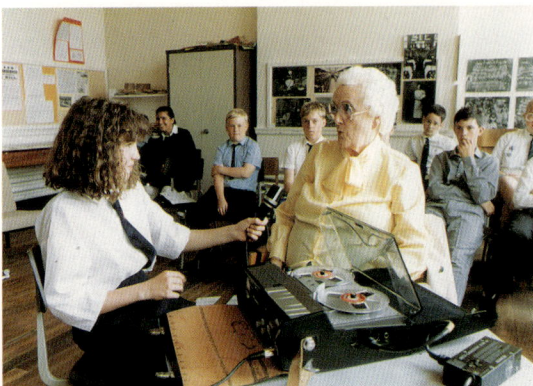

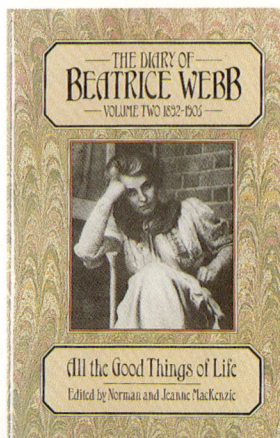

THE DIARY OF
BEATRICE WEBB
— VOLUME TWO 1832-1905 —

All the Good Things of Life
Edited by Norman and Jeanne MacKenzie

It is quite likely that the writer will gather all the information he or she thinks is useful in a card index. This might be divided up into sections such as those shown here.

Write

Once the writer has a feeling for the period, he or she will begin to work on devising the story, working the information collected to give a real feeling for the period like Roger Green does. Using your notes now try to draft a plot for your story based on the sources at the bottom of pp. 108–9.

Research and write

To finish this section try using your research to write a story set in a time in history that interests you. It might be set in any time such as Roman Britain, or even during the Second World War. You decide.

Once you have decided, begin researching the period in the way described above and using the approach set out on pp. 102–3. During your research do not just collect details about the period, try to develop an idea of how the people of the time thought and behaved so that the reader can really believe your characters existed.

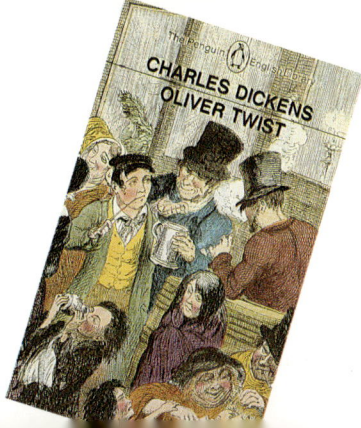

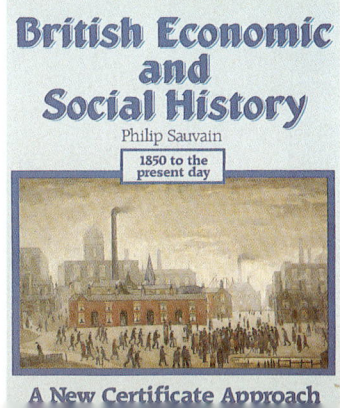

BELIEFS

T.V.
TOP OF THE POPS
DOCTOR WHO?
SGT. BILKO

FASHION

MUSIC

SCIENCE/TRAVEL

LIVING

INTERESTS

HIPPIES
LOVE

TRANSPORT

MONEY
2/6d   3/6d   4/9d

CHARLES DICKENS
OLIVER TWIST

British Economic and Social History
Philip Sauvain
1850 to the present day

A New Certificate Approach

MODULE 6 WRITING

Mapping writerland

Introduction

In Module 3: Writing (p. 39) you began to keep a writer's log to help you develop your own awareness of the problems and successes you have as a writer, in all your school subjects. You also concentrated on narrative writing, the making of stories.

In this module you will be looking at the variety of different forms of writing, how these change depending on audience, purpose and form, and trying some of them out.

You should still find time to write entries in your log, to keep a record of your progress.

1 Stormy weather

Read and discuss

Sunday Evening. We have had a dreadful storm of wind in the forepart of this day, which has done a great deal of mischief among our trees. I was sitting alone in the dining room, when an odd kind of crash startled me – in a moment afterwards it was repeated; I then went to the window, which I reached just in time to see the last of our two highly valued Elms descend into the Sweep!!! The other, which had fallen I suppose in the first crash, & which was the nearest to the pond, taking a more easterly direction sunk amongst our screen of chestnuts and firs, knocking down one spruce fir, beating off the head of another, and stripping the two corner chestnuts in its fall. This is not all.

With your partner, discuss these questions about this letter:
▶ Was the writer writing to a friend or relative?
▶ What clues did you find for your answer?
▶ Was the writer poor or rich?
▶ How did you decide this answer?
▶ Did the writer live in a town or in the country?
▶ Can you find any clues which help you with this question?
▶ What facts does the writer give her reader? List them.

Letters tell you a lot about the writer, and about the **purpose** of writing.

When you write a letter you can choose your language patterns; this means you can decide which **words** to use, what groups to make of them, and what sort of **sentences** to use. Your choices will have an effect on the reader of the letter.

Look back to pp. 34–6 to check on audience, purpose and form in writing letters.

LANGUAGE NOTE

You have just looked at a letter Jane Austen wrote to her sister. She is able to be chatty; she does not have to explain things like the 'Sweep'; she can mention the 'screen of chestnuts and firs' as 'ours'. She shares knowledge of the house and garden with her sister.

So the variety of language, or *register*, **she is able to use, is different from the variety she might use to an insurance company, in making a claim for damages caused by the storm. Compare the need for every detail to be explained in the accident report below.**

Variety is the key to successful writing. You need to be able to use many different registers, in different subjects and different situations, as you go through school and after you have left. You are just starting to develop an awareness of what you have to do. Make entries in your log about different registers of writing. Try to focus on which are most difficult, which easiest, and why.

Discuss, improvise and write

At the end of the extract from Jane Austen's letter, the words 'This is not all' appear. With a partner, discuss what else might have happened. Remember she was living on the edge of a village; other people might have been involved in the storm.

Decide on a role; you could be a farm worker, a landowner, a thief, a parson, a poor child, a rich child, a landlord/landlady, a doctor. Improvise a dialogue which tells more of the story of the storm. Record it on a cassette. Listen to your dialogue and then turn it into a letter to a friend.

▶ What changes did you find you had to make to do this?
▶ How did your understanding of audience, purpose and form guide your writing?

LANGUAGE NOTE

Language forms are made to change when the *purpose* **and** *audience* **change. Look at these road signs. They are as short as they could be. Why? Now read this eyewitness report of a road accident.**

'I was sitting in my car, which was parked facing south on Wells Road, on the eastern side about ten metres north of the Top Shop. Outside the Top Shop facing south a grey Volvo saloon was parked. A blue car, make unknown, parked opposite the Top Shop, facing north partially on the pavement. A Ford Escort travelling south at 25–30 mph overtook my car. At the same time a car approached from the south at 35–40mph hit the Ford Escort, which had braked sharply, and knocked it into the Volvo. At the time of the accident the weather was wet, the visibility very poor. It occurred at 4.30 p.m. on 1.2.90.'

What can you say about the language forms in this report? What purpose is it written for? Who do you think the audience might be?

▶ THINK ABOUT WHO YOU'RE WRITING FOR, WHAT THE PURPOSE OF WRITING IS, AND HOW YOU ARE GOING TO DO IT.

2 Stormy weather – twentieth-century style

Jane Austen lived when there was no electricity, gas, telephone, TV, radio, cars, planes or trains. Even in the 1990s, with all the technology we have, a storm can be terrifying and destructive. In 1987 there was a violent storm over Southern England. Here are some pieces of writing about the storm and its effects on some of the people who were involved in it.

Read and discuss

1 'The hurricane attacked in waves starting with a faraway growl and building up to a frightening roar as it blasted everything in its path. The roar drowned the crunch of falling trees. It drowned the sound of tiles and slates being ripped away. Limbs from trees flew in the air and petrified animals instinctively sought shelter in young coppices away from the swaying giants. . . . Gravestones were lifted in cemeteries, headstones smashed and crosses cracked. Dinghies and boats in reservoirs and lakes were thrown together in a giant's junk yard scene. The M4 was brought to a standstill with the elevated section in West London closed. The M25 was blocked in many places. Many towns and villages were completely cut off. Airports closed and trains came to a standstill.'

2 'Suddenly there was the most terrifying earsplitting crash. Wendy saw the light of dawn open above her. Briefly there was sky and then darkness again as roof tiles, masonry, jagged branches, plaster and rubble rained on top of her.

Wendy writes "Even today I can hear my own screams and remember how I instinctively found the strength to remove great weights and scramble free."'

3 'At 9.00 p.m. on Thursday evening, October 15 1987 a depression (low) of central pressure 972 millibars was centred over the north of East Anglia. From this depression a frontal zone lay across the south of England to another depression which was believed to be centred over the western entrance to the English Channel with a central pressure less than 966 millibars.'

4 'It was nearly four in the morning, and like most of Sussex, I was sound asleep. The telephone; "Fiona, this is newsdesk. There's a bit of a gale out there and you're the only one able to reach Worthing office. We still want to piece together a paper and need early copy."'

From *In the Wake of the Hurricane*, Bob Ogley

▶ DIFFERENT KINDS OF WRITING MAKE DIFFERENT DEMANDS ON THE READER. THEY ALSO NEED DIFFERENT FORMS AND STYLES.

In groups, talk about the four extracts. Discuss the purpose of each one. Ask yourselves these questions:

▶ Does it give straight information?
▶ Can you spot any words or phrases in the language of these extracts which stand out? Try extract 3 first.
▶ What happens to the language about halfway through extract 1? Does it change the way you read the passage?
▶ How many words to do with damage caused by the hurricane can you find? Which extract has most in and why?
▶ Is the phrase 'bit of a gale' (extract 4) a joke? If you think it is, what clues can you find from the other extracts to prove it?

Your answers should show you that writers make choices in their writing for different purposes. They have to think about why they are writing the particular piece, who is going to read it, and what the best choices of style and form will be.

③ Eyes and 'I's

In extracts 2 and 4 on the storm (p. 112) you saw two examples of personal narrative. This is when the writer uses 'I'. You tried some of this sort of storytelling on p. 6. But that was slightly different, because you transcribed a spoken story. What is it like to **write** a personal account?

Nella Last was a middle-aged woman living in Barrow-in-Furness in the north-west of England, in 1939 when war was declared with Germany. She had a husband and two sons. During the war she kept a diary. She had volunteered to do this so that people in the future, like you, could find out about ordinary people's lives in the 1930s and 1940s. Here are some extracts from her personal account of her experiences and feelings, and the experiences of the people of Barrow.

Wednesday, 6 November, 1940

. . . Four of them had white tablecloths on their heads and their caps on top, and they walked heavily, singing a dreary tune with what sounded like 'La La La' recurring frequently. As I turned, I found several more perched insecurely on a wall and said, 'Aren't you afraid of falling? Come and run about, and keep warm. Then I saw the heap of wicked-looking stones, and saw they each had stones in their hands ready to throw. I said, 'What are you playing now?' and got the eager answer, 'I'm Mussy and this is Bruno, and we are waiting to bomb the pilgrims when they come underneath, and then the soldiers will fight us.' I looked at the stones and said, 'What a pity you have no nice 'real' bombs. Come round with me and I'll make you some *beauties* – and give you a bomb-carrier.' I left my poppy-selling and we hurried round. I got out my rag-bag, and in a few minutes had a pile of bombs the size of an orange, made of winceyette cuttings tied up in scraps of dark material, and off they went with their harmless load.

I was tired out when I got in, and when I took my shoes off, felt too lazy to go to get my slippers, so I sat with my stockinged feet stretched out. That suited my little animals fine. Mr. Murphy curled close to one foot and my old faithful Sol laid his grizzled head on the other, and we all felt content by the fire. My husband and I discussed our new shelter, and have got all settled. He is going to reinforce under the stairs, and I'll put a single bed and roll of bedding in. At a pinch we could both sleep on it.

Friday, 8 November, 1940

It's the custom for fish and fruit shops in Barrow to print their special lines on the outside windows with a small brush dipped in whitening: '*SPECIAL*! RABBITS. CRABS.' The better-class shops *never* do, and I was really amused by one such shop today, for on both windows – it's on a corner – was printed neatly and in extra large letters:

NO EGGS
NO LEMONS
NO ONIONS
NO LEEKS
NO PAPER BAGS

I wondered how many times Mrs. Jones had had to say those words before, in exasperation, she printed them on the window. The fishmonger's shop was quite nicely stocked – especially with rabbits. I got one and paid 1s. 8d. Considering the time of year, I thought they were an indifferent sample – I like to see pale pink flesh and the kidneys sunk in creamy fat. I hunted well through the furry rows, and did not feel so suited with what I got finally.

Rations had been cut. The sugar allowance was now only eight ounces a week, tea two ounces, and margarine as well as cooking fats joined butter on the ration-books. The production of such things as cups, cutlery, kettles, clocks, furniture, toys and prams had been severely curtailed as 'inessentials', while such 'luxury' goods as ball-cocks for lavatories, pencils, gardening implements and needles became unobtainable in many areas. What luxuries there were, such as cosmetics, were now subject to a thirty-three per cent purchase tax.

Friday, 9 May, 1941

People have been sleeping in hedges and fields all round the outside of town – no one has *any* faith in shelters. After the first small attack, when people died in bed and amid their ruined homes and the shelters stood up unharmed, practically all deaths have been in shelters when houses crashed on them. In the centre of town last night it was dreadful, for after the bombs started to fall and crash, the poor things rushed from the little box-like back street shelters into their houses, and then out into the street again – frantic with fear and not knowing where to go. We have no really decent public shelters. I don't think our Council ever really thought we would 'get it' – in fact, I don't think many people did.

There were public shelters in Barrow for only 3,500 people out of a population of 70,000. As a direct result of the Blitz, 83 people were killed, 330 injured, and 10,000 houses were damaged.

Saturday, 10 May, 1941

Last night started off so terribly that, if it had gone on, there would have been little of Barrow left. Pieces of railway rails and slates seemed everywhere this morning, and the sky was red with fire. There was a lull in the barrage, then we heard a plane or planes from another direction and the raiders were chased out to sea. Ruth called in to say there had been a lot of damage to streets and the Yard again, and people were being dug out of shelters again. She spoke of Thursday's damage to the Yard, when men were trapped for a while in the deep shelters. She said Gerald – her sweetheart – had not spoken all day, and then his mother had coaxed him to talk and get it out of his system. Ruth said that the men took cover as usual, and as usual played cards by torchlight and sat and talked – mostly doubtful jokes and stories and, in the hardboiled way of Yard workers, they cursed and blasphemed. After one frightful crash, when a large crane came down, the foreman went to see the damage and came back and said, 'I hope to God there is not another – it looks as if we are trapped now.' As he spoke there was a worse crump, and then a deathly silence. Gerald said torches dropped from nerveless

fingers on to the floor, and by their light he saw the 'round' of knees as men instinctively dropped to kneel on playing cards or newspapers. He saw clenched or clasped hands and a glimpse of grey hollowed cheeks, and then a calm steady voice rose, 'Father, into thy hands we commend our spirits,' and the Lord's Prayer started. Gerald recognised the voice as belonging to about the dirtiest-mouthed and hardest-swearing man in the shop – a footballer. Above their heads, the layer of concrete cracked and shifted with the weight of piling machinery, flung in a heap by the blast; and then a wide crack appeared on the side of the shelter, and light showed through. They managed to scramble out and all were saved – as if by a miracle, for the floor of the shop caved in on to their shelter shortly afterwards.

Armour-piercing shells wrecked two streets near the docks, and more general damage was done. What would have happened if Spitfires had not come, one trembles to think. Barrow is so small that we are 'all in it together', and it's so dreadful when people have no confidence in their brick shelters. I bless the impulse that made my husband decide, after weeks of consideration, to send for our iron indoor shelter, where we can go to bed and feel reasonably safe.

Few seemed to be going to sleep in Barrow, if the cars and buses were any guide, and a steady trek without break stretched for miles as we came from Spark Bridge. Gone is all the weariness and age from that little old Aunt of mine. Instead, there is a bustling busy person, with grey hair like a last-year's bird's nest, sleeves rolled up above the elbow, preparing soup and vegetables for tomorrow, getting out every possible cover and pillow, and considering at every moment the best course to pursue. My husband said, 'You're a queer lot – you actually seem to *like* danger and upset. I've never seen you work so hard, or seen you so cheerful for years – and on less food and sleep at that!'

Sunday, 1 August, 1943

I suddenly thought tonight, 'I know why a lot of women have gone into pants – it's a sign that they are asserting themselves in some way.' I feel pants are more of a sign of the times than I realised. A growing contempt for man in general creeps over me. For a craftsman, whether a sweep or Prime Minister – 'hats off'. But why this 'Lords of Creation' attitude on men's part? I'm beginning to see I'm a really clever woman in my own line, and not the 'odd' or 'uneducated' woman that I've had dinned into me. Not that in-laws have bothered me for some time now. I got on my top note, and swept all clean, after one stick bit of interference and bother. I feel that, in the world of tomorrow, marriage will be – will *have* to be – more of a partnership, less of this 'I have spoken' attitude. They will talk things over – talking *does* do good, if only to clear the air. I run my house like a business: I have had to, to get all done properly, everything fitted in. Why, then, should women not be looked on as partners, as 'business women'? I feel thoroughly out of time. I'm not as patient as I used to be, and when one gets to fifty-three, and after thirty-two years of married life, there are few illusions to cloud issues.

Nella Last's War

Read and discuss

With a partner, read the extracts from *Nella Last's War*. Think about her problems in choosing what to write about. You could focus on the following points:
▶ How children's games became dangerous.
▶ How people lived without lots of things you expect to have today.
▶ What the bombs did to Barrow.
▶ How people reacted to the bombing.

▶ How Nella Last felt when she described the air raids.
▶ How Nella Last's ideas about herself changed.
▶ How the choices of language in the extracts show differences between descriptions and feelings – look at the writer's use of 'I' and her choice of verbs to start you off.
▶ What words or phrases show the writing is from the 1940s.

Research

Nella Last wrote about her changing feelings concerning marriage and how women should be equal partners in a marriage. As a class, you are going to find out if family life has changed since the 1940s.
▶ Make a list of activities which are necessary to keep a household running smoothly.
▶ Make a bar graph or pie chart to show who does each activity in everyone's home. If you are not sure how to do this ask your maths teacher.
▶ With the help of your history teacher, find out more about family life in the Second World War.

▶ Make a wall chart displaying all your results. On your wall chart you should decide how best to present your information, in consultation with your teacher. You could think about these questions:
  - What sections does the chart need?
  - Should the information be a mixture of words and photographs?
  - Should anyone do any graphic work for the chart?
  - What does the reader need to find out from the chart?
You could head it 'Family Life 1940–91'.

Discuss

In pairs, look at some photographs from the Second World War. Discuss what you learn from these photos and then compare that with what you learned from Nella Last's writing. Try to pinpoint the differences between the way photos give you information, and how writing does.

HOW DOES PERSONAL WRITING REACH OUT TO READERS? WHAT WAS THE SECOND WORLD WAR LIKE FOR WOMEN LIKE NELLA LAST? HAVE THINGS CHANGED?

Writing

Over to you. Think back over the last week. What has been happening in your street, town or village?

Just like Nella Last, keep a diary so that other people can have a record of life in your home area. Write two entries for the last week.

Guidelines:

▶ Do the first draft, not the polished final version.
▶ Remember to make clear any details of places a reader might not know about.
▶ You can put in your feelings as well as describing things or events.
▶ If you are stuck, get some ideas from the local paper or radio station.
▶ It is your eyes the readers are going to see through – you are a camera.
▶ Write in Standard English as far as you can.

Discuss

When you have completed the first draft, talk about it with a partner. Decide if each of you have succeeded in the task and make alterations if you agree with your partner's suggestions. Focus closely on the language choices each of you made. When you have completed the final version the class could make a wall display of the diary entries.

John Evelyn

Research

In pairs, find out some information about other diaries. They might be modern, like Anne Frank's or they might be from another century like Samuel Pepys'. Make notes on what the writers put in their diaries, and try to spot and note down any differences in language from modern English. Note down also the differences in the way people live as shown in the diaries.

Here is an example from the diaries of John Evelyn who lived from 1620 to 1706.

June, the next morning finding my-selfe extreamly, & beaten with my Journey, I went to one of their Bagnias, which are made, & treate after the Eastern manner, washing one with hot & cold water, with oyles, rubbing with a kind of Strigil, which a naked youth puts on his hand like a glove of seales Skin, or what ever it be, fetching off a world of dirt, & stretching out ones limbs, then claps on a depilatorie made of a drug or earth they call Resina, that comes out of Turky, which takes off all the haire of the body, as resin dos a piggs.

Make some notes on any difficulties you had reading that extract. What differences between modern English and John Evelyn's English can you find? Is the spelling the same? Are the sentence forms the same?

Both John Evelyn and Nella Last were writing personal accounts of their lives and experiences for other people to read.

Sometimes diaries are written only for the writer, and then the choice of language pattern does not have to involve the idea of an audience.

Presentation

The Secret Diary of Adrian Mole aged $13\frac{3}{4}$ is a fictional diary written as if it was a secret personal account.

Read the following page from a comic strip take-off of Adrian Mole. What would you change if you were writing the storyline to present to a reader who was going to test your spelling?

The Sekret Diary ov Hadrian Vile - Aged 8⅝ (years)

I wotched an intresting program about shepperds...

Soe I deesided to trane Bowser as a shepe-dog, and tuk him to the parck...

Come by, Bowser! Good boy!

PARK →

Snickers!

I dident have annie shepe for him to rownd up, butt I'de gott sum froggs that I'de hatched from froggs-pawn...

Unforchoonatelie, Bowser woz useless at shepe-dogging...

Sproing!

Boing!

Ribit!

Sum of the frogs escayped into the gent's toylet, and the park-keeper woz in there at the tyme!

Aaiee!

GENTS

The froggs gayve him a reel frite, and it tuck him a wile to get them orl out of his trowsis...

Bye whitch tyme, othar peeple had startid complayning...

The parkie mayde me round up orl the froggs, which tuck ayges...

Excuse me!

Then he mayde a new "park rool"...
Whitch left me feeling pritty shepe-ish!

PARK NOTICE FROGS ALL DOGS MUST BE KEPT ON A LEAD

RODGERS/JACKSON

A really crucial guide to...

Spelling 2

In your writing, the final edit is crucial to good presentation. Here are some more guidelines for your spelling success.

The spelling game

Play this game in groups.

1 One member of the group choose a word, puts a dash for each letter of the word, and writes in the first letter. So, for 'market' he or she would write: m _ _ _ _ _ .

2 The rest of the group have ten guesses for each letter. If they have not guessed a letter after the tenth guess. Leave it blank and go on to the next letter.

They must guess the letters in their correct order in the word. To guess 'm(arket)' they must go from a to t in strict sequence – a r k e t. Do not leave letters blank without having ten guesses first.

3 The first person to guess what the word is chooses the next word.

Make a note of the spelling of key words that you need to remember for other subjects, such as science, history, geography or technology (ask your teachers if necessary). Use these words when it is your turn to choose a word, or look for difficult words that will baffle your friends.

Word look-alikes

One of the problems of spelling in English is that some words look alike but have different sounds when they are spoken.

'Lead' and 'Lead' have the same spelling but two meanings. If you see 'Lead me away from here' in a book, 'Lead' is a process word, or **verb** which means 'guide' or 'direct'. But if you see 'Lead was stolen from the church roof last night' in a newspaper, 'Lead' is the name of a soft metal.

Make your own lists of word look-alikes. They are usually called **homonyms**, but a better name for them would be **homographs**. See if you can find out why.

Word sound-alikes

Bare, bear, there, their, hair, hare . . . You can add to this list very easily, I expect. This group of words is made up of pairs or threes which sound alike. But you spell them differently, and they all have different meanings. Words in this group are usually called **homophones**.

Make your own list of word sound-alikes.

Some spelling rules

When you write you are using the rules of the writing system. Spelling is always a visual pattern which you can see in words on a page, or on a screen. Here are some rules which you could use to help your own spelling become better:

▶ Think about how words are built up, especially those used in other subjects.

▶ Look carefully at words. See if you can spot patterns in the letters which you know of in other words – for example, 'globe', 'global' and 'globule' all have 'glob' as their basic pattern.

▶ Try to see words with your eyes shut! Make the words walk on the inside of your eyelids!

▶ When you learn a word: **Look at it, Cover it up, Write it down, Check it.**

▶ Try always to remember a word before you write it down.

▶ Try! Do not give up. Your spelling will get better if you have a go.

▶ Be careful about your handwriting. If you have problems with it, ask your teacher for help.

▶ Play with word patterns on a wordprocessor.

▶ Make some crosswords, using groups of words with the same letter patterns in, for younger children to solve.

There will be more spelling advice and help in Book Two.

4 Finding a voice

> HOW DOES A SCRIPT WRITER MAKE A SCRIPT WORK? HOW CAN YOU FIND A VOICE FOR YOUR WORDS?

Nella Last wrote about her feelings changing towards men. She had begun to realise that she had strengths of her own, and that she was not going to be the underdog any more.

Discuss and improvise

In groups, discuss how family life is portrayed in your favourite TV soap opera.

Consider the following questions:
▶ Do the male characters and the female characters have different roles in the TV family?
▶ Do any characters behave in a way that could threaten the TV family?
▶ How do arguments get sorted out in the TV family?

Now improvise a scene from an imaginary soap opera which you have created.
Focus on:
▶ who the main characters are
▶ what they do
▶ who is powerful, who is weak
▶ how each character uses language suitable for his/ her position in the soap.

To get you started, look back at the sample plot planner on p. 13.

Read and discuss

You have been exploring the ways in which language defines a character in a soap opera. Now read this extract from *Up to you, Porky*, a TV comedy sketch. Discuss the way language is used:
▶ for humour
▶ to control the situation
▶ to show who is winning.

Cleaning

A large, messy, stripped-pine kitchen. Ursula, a large messy lady novelist in a smock sits drinking tea with Kent, a disdainful Northern man.

Ursula You know, it's amazing: you're the only person who's answered the advert. I just cannot get a cleaner. I'm afraid it's all rather neglected in here.

Kent Well, yes, I was just admiring that blue mink hat, but I see now it's a mouldy pizza.

Ursula I'm a novelist, and it's so hard to do everything. Is the tea all right?

Kent Not really.

Ursula Oh sorry, is it too strong?

Kent I'm just a bit perturbed by the way it's taken the tarnish off this teaspoon.

Ursula Biscuit?

Kent Have they got chemicals in?

Ursula Preservatives?

Kent I was hoping for disinfectant.

Ursula No, I baked them myself.

Kent I bet Mr Kipling's worried.

Ursula Aren't you going to finish it?

Kent I'll keep it by me – you never know, I may need to force a lock.
Pause
Anyone ever told you you've got a look of Molly Weir?

Ursula No.

Kent I'm not surprised.

Ursula Have you been a cleaner for long?

Kent Well, I was abroad for some years.

Ursula Really?

From *Up to you, Porky*, Victoria Wood

LANGUAGE NOTE

Using language is not always as easy. To find your own voice, to speak and write the way you want is often a struggle against the voices and words of others. Whenever you use language, you are in a situation of words and meanings which do not always belong to you. You may feel that other people are controlling what you can say, or write. In pairs, brainstorm a list of situations where you can be put under pressure to use language as

others want you to. How does this idea link up with the writer's need to think about audience, purpose and form/style? If you do not have many ideas about this yet, put it in your log as a problem to consider carefully for future work.

Read, discuss and perform

In groups, read the extracts from a *Fawlty Towers* script. The characters' names have been deleted from the script, but are listed here.

Basil Fawlty, owner of Fawlty Towers Hotel
Mr Johnson, a guest
Mrs Yolande Johnson, his wife
Ronald Johnson, their son

Copy out the extract so that each group has one copy. Discuss who should be speaking each speech: for example, if you think Basil says 'I don't like the chips', write his name against the words. Like this:

    BASIL   I don't like the chips.

Do this for each speech. Then take parts and read them aloud. Try varying the intonation and volume of your voice till you are satisfied with your performance.

When you have done this, discuss the ways in which different characters used language choices to try to control the situation.

Basil smiles balefully.

_____ Oh dear. What's er . . . what's wrong with them then?
_____ They're the wrong shape and they're just awful.
_____ I'm afraid he gets everything cooked the way he likes it, at home.
_____ Does he, does he?
_____ Yes I do, and it's better than this pig's garbage.
_____ (*slightly amused*) Now Ronald.
_____ These eggs look like you laid them.
_____ (*to Ronald, friendlily*) Now look here old boy . . .
_____ Shut up!! Leave him alone! (*She turns to Basil*) He's very clever, rather highly strung.
_____ Yes, yes, he should be.

Ronald fixes Basil contemptuously.

_____ Haven't you got any proper chips?
_____ Well these <u>are</u> proper French Fried Potatoes. You see, our <u>chef</u> . . . is <u>Continental</u>.
_____ Couldn't you get an English one?

Basil is momentarily stumped. Yolande laughs. Basil's eyes move to her.

_____ But hasn't he got any of the frozen crinkly ones?
_____ I'm afraid he hasn't.
_____ Oh!?
_____ Why not!?
_____ Well, he likes cooking. That's why he became a chef.
_____ (*to Ronald*) Why don't you eat just one or two dear?
_____ They're the wrong shape.
_____ (*solicitously*) What shape do you usually have? Micky Mouse shape? Smarties shape? Amphibious landing craft shape? Poke in the eye shape?
_____ . . . God, you're <u>dumb</u>.

Ronald appraises him.

_____ Oh, now . . .

Basil is holding himself on a very tight rein.

_____ Well is there something you'd like instead, <u>Sonny</u>?
_____ . . . I'd like some bread and salad cream.
_____ To <u>eat</u>? Well . . . (*he points*) there's the bread, and there's the mayonnaise.
_____ I said <u>salad</u> <u>cream</u>, stupid.
_____ We <u>don't</u> <u>have</u> salad cream. The chef made <u>this</u> (*indicating mayonnaise*) <u>fresh</u> this morning.
_____ What a dump!
_____ (*offering Ronald the mayonnaise*) This is <u>very</u> <u>good</u>.
_____ He likes salad cream.
_____ (*to Basil, pointing at the mayonnaise*). That's puke that is.
_____ Well at least it's fresh puke, ha ha!
_____ (*shocked*) Oh dear!!
_____ (*indignantly*) Well <u>he</u> said it!
_____ (*loftily*) May I ask why you don't have any proper salad cream. I mean most restaurants . . .
_____ Well our chef only buys it on special occasions, you know, gourmet nights and so on, but . . . <u>when</u> he's got a bottle he's a genius with it. He can unscrew the top like Robert Carrier. It's a treat to watch (*he mimes*).
_____ <u>Right</u> on the plate.

Getting a grip on words is not always easy. The words have been used by other people before you began to speak or write. Read the extract from *Crummy Mummy and Me*. Decide who is in control and how the writer uses language, both words and groups of words to make you, the reader, think about Minna's and Crummy Mummy's relationship.

I didn't know I was going to be *that* late, did I? And there was absolutely no need at all for Mr Russell to say in quite so waspish a tone of voice:

"I've had quite enough of this, Minna! Last week you said you had a dental appointment and disappeared for the entire afternoon. On Monday you turned up so tired I could see the bags under your eyes. Today you're horribly late and, on top of everything, you've even forgotten to bring in your Elk Money! Now I'm going to send a note home with you today, asking your mother to come in to school tomorrow morning and have a little chat about things."

My eyes must have gone as round as saucers. I simply couldn't think what good he thought talking to my Crummy Mummy would do!

But there's no accounting for teachers, so I just kept quiet.

I did try to get Mum to dress sensibly for the meeting, though.

"*Not* the angora top with the puff sleeves and the low bosom," I told her. "And *not* the purple, scalloped wellies. *Not* the plastic viper necklace. And *no* yellow eye-shadow. *Please*, Mum."

Mum put her head inside a Tesco paper bag.

"I suppose you'd like me to go in to school like this," she said.

"That's nice," said Crusher Maggot. "That really suits you."

I sighed. At times it's like living with two small children, honestly it is.

I did what I could. I hid some of the worst of her clothes and jewellery, and set my alarm clock for half an hour earlier the following morning. As soon as I was dressed, I went and stood in the doorway watching her sternly while she chose her clothes. She knew I meant business. She saw the steely look in my eyes. She didn't argue. When we walked into school, she looked practically normal.

"Right," I warned her between gritted teeth. "Whatever he says, *whatever*, nod and agree! Promise?"

"Promise," said Mum. (Credit where credit's due, she does mean well.)

Mr Russell clearly thought so, anyhow. He was quite taken with her. They spent a lot of time together, laughing and chatting outside the staffroom door. I peeped down the corridor twice, and both times Mum

was obediently nodding. Mr Russell was so bewitched he even handed her his morning cup of coffee, the one he says he needs so badly he'd have to prop his eyelids apart with matchsticks if he didn't get it. And when he finally came back, alone, into the classroom, he leaned over my desk and whispered in my ear.

"*What* a nice Mum you have, Minna! Very cooperative. She's so prepared to be helpful that when I asked if she'd come on the Friday field trip to the zoo to see Elsie our elk, she nodded and agreed."

I buried my head in my hands. I could have *wept*.

We had a blazing row about it when I got home.

"Why did you say that?" I shouted at her. "Why did you say you would come with us to the zoo on Friday? You know you won't. You can't *bear* zoos. So you know you can't go. When Mr Russell invited you on the trip, why did you simply *nod and agree*?"

"But that's exactly what you *told* me to do, Minna!" she retorted. "That's what you made me promise! *Nod and agree*!"

"But not to go to the zoo!"

"*Whatever*, you said. Whatever he says, nod and agree!"

Sometimes I feel like despairing, truly I do.

"But what on earth will we do when Friday comes?"

"We'll think of something between us."

"Well, let's think *now*."

So we all sat there, thinking. And it was Crusher who came up trumps. He said to Mum:

"Why don't you send Gran along in your place? She likes zoos a lot. She can tell Mr Russell that Crummy Dummy kept sneezing, so you thought you should keep her at home, and she has come to help instead."

I know a good idea when I hear it.

"Brilliant!" I enthused. Gran is great fun. She'd make any visit to a zoo a treat, and everyone in my class would like her.

"Brilliant!" Mum agreed. She was relieved. She hadn't wanted to let anyone down.

"Brilliant!" echoed Crusher. (He's never been overburdened with modesty, our Crusher.)

And I was satisfied.

From *Crummy Mummy and Me*, Anne Fines

5 Only smarties have the answer

Because we live in groups, such as families and societies, there are always pressures from other people to persuade us to behave in this or that way, or to buy this or that wonderful gadget. People use language cleverly to persuade and control us.

Discuss

In groups, make a list of things which you buy. For each thing identify an advertisement from TV or comics or magazines which is trying to sell it. Pick out the five most interesting advertisements and discuss why they work. Focus on:

▶ the words of the advertisement – are they clever? Do they make you laugh?
▶ the images or pictures of the advertisement – how do they persuade you?
▶ whether the advertisement describes the product accurately.

What are your favourite slogans or punchlines in advertisements? Why do you like them? In your groups, list your top ten.

Now take one word from each slogan and change it to change the meaning of the whole slogan. Here is an example:

The smoothest creamiest flakiest chocolate in the world

becomes

The smoothest crummiest flakiest chocolate in the world

Sometimes advertisers have to change the names of the products they are trying to sell. The Marathon chocolate bar became Snickers in 1990 because in Europe its name was Snickers.

Now try to find five things which you think might be very difficult to sell. Each group should decide on one thing and produce an advertisement for it. Remember that in advertisements, the ideas of audience, purpose and form/style are researched very hard, so that people can be persuaded to buy the product. Try to choose words which will persuade *your* buyers.

To give you some ideas here is a joke advertisement from a comic.

Natlays
The Piggy Bank

Wow! How incredibly swinging and groovy! Hey, kids – wouldn't you love to have your very own PSYCHEDELIC bank account, just like the oldies do, but specially designed to TODAY'S KIDS? Gosh-o-matic, you certainly would!

For an initial deposit of just £100, here's what you get:

$ Nothing!
$ Absolutely nothing!
$ No things!
$ Not a sausage!

PLUS!!

Absolutely free – a truly FAB lime-green fluorescent floppy plastic holder to keep it all in!! Howsabout that then, GUYS'N'GALS??

ALL YOU HAVE TO DO:

Give us the dosh. Sign a crazy piece of paper promising to give us any other dosh you may ever own for the rest of your life. AND THEN – forget all about it! That's right, we'll take care of everything, cos we know zany kids aren't interested in borin' ol' money – right?? Course we're right!! Kids just wanna have fun!!

And don't forget, all young investors are authorised to sing Natlays very own hip, teen-style "wrap" song:

"Banks ain't boring, they ain't glum,
No! Banks are – um, dumdy dumdy dum.
So get down to the bank and give 'em all your BREAD,
or they'll send a big lion round to bite off your HEAD!!
– Sir Matthew Coward-Thief,
Investment Manager (and a really "together" dude!)

This has been a GBH Madvertisement.

BEFORE YOU WRITE, DISCUSS HOW THE NATLAYS ADVERTISEMENT COMPARES WITH TEENAGE REGISTERS WHICH YOU LOOKED AT ON PAGES 36–7.

Writing

Imagine you have to persuade some unfriendly aliens that you are a really great person. You do not have to tell them anything bad about you, but you must make them aware of all your good points. Write your advertisement for yourself.

▶ Choose your words carefully – do not just write the first word that comes into your head.
▶ Remember to think about making your good qualities crystal clear, so do not write 'I am quite good at writing.' Show how good

you are by, for example, writing, 'I can write very clear business letters, inspiring poems, and exciting short stories'.

⑥ It's my life

We all start life in some particular place. Some of us move house, or country; some of us live in the same area all our lives. So when people write **autobiographies** they often mention where they first lived. What is an autobiography? It is the story someone writes about herself or himself. Lots of autobiographies are by famous people, but anyone can write one.

Read and discuss

Read the extracts from autobiographies printed on pp. 124–7. With your partner, discuss how each writer presents him or herself. Focus on:
▶ what the writer chooses to write about
▶ how the writer expresses feelings through choosing words and sentences
▶ difficulties for the reader because he or she does not know the writer
▶ where the writing becomes interesting to you.

MY FIRST MEMORIES

The thing that sticks in my mind most from when I was very young is the first time I stole something; I was about two years old at the time. My mother and I were visiting friends who had some older children who had practically every toy under the sun because they had rich relatives who spoilt them. Anyway, even at such an early age I wondered why they could have so many lovely toys when all I had was a few cars, a teddy bear and a bedraggled old doll. So I decided that I would have some of their toys. I remember picking out the things that would not be missed, and I stuffed them behind the pillow in my pram which was very easy to climb into. When it was time to go home, my mum told me to get into the pram, but I refused. So I walked home. When we got home I started taking the toys out. My mum was very angry and brought me back with the toys. I had to say sorry, and I remember feeling very resentful because I thought it just was not fair – they had everything they wanted, and I didn't.

I was, and still am, up to a point, very close to my father. He was not soft with me as a child. He was always firm but fair. If he thought I needed a good slap then I'd get one or two but he would never ever over do it. Every weekend he would bring home a large bag of sweets to my brother and myself if we were good. He said he had a horse-friend and a squirrel who spied on us when he was at work, to see we were behaving ourselves. Then they would meet him on his way home and give him the report. My brother and myself always wondered how he knew what we had done that day. We really believed he did have a horse and a squirrel friend. We did not realise that it was our mum who was the horse and squirrel. But if we fought we knew we need not expect any sweets.

As a child I was terribly jealous of my brother. Ever since mum first brought him home I hated him. Mum left me with the friends I have already mentioned. She was a long time in hospital because she had to have a special operation for John to be born (Caesarian). Anyway I did not remember her after such a long time and I was calling the lady I was staying with, Mummy, instead. I was really shocked when I was brought home again to find someone else had 'taken my place'. As soon as I saw John I scratched him across his face and every chance I got afterwards I hit him with all my strength.

I was never really all that much interested in doll's houses and mini-ironing boards and cookers and silly things like dressing up in wimmin's clothes and high heels and all the things that most little girls are conditioned to do. My mother did not really believe in putting me into frilly frocks and snow white socks. I nearly always wore trousers and 'boys' clothes. My brother laughs when he sees me in these clothes in old photos but I don't see anything 'wrong' or funny about girls wearing 'boys' clothes.

Religion played quite a big role in my childhood. As we are a Roman Catholic family we went to church every Sunday morning. My parents taught John and myself to say our prayers every night before we went to bed. They encouraged us to believe that God was very important and that he was to be thought of with the highest respect. As a child I always wondered what God looked like.

When my grandmother and grandfather died (my mother's parents) I knew I should feel sad but I didn't.

I must have been too young to realise. I remember my mother was very sad especially as they died within 10 months of each other. I did not know my grandparents very well as they lived in Ireland even though we went to visit them almost every year.

I remember my granny as a fat womin with a nice kind face. She always wore a blue dress with red flowers in it. My grandad was tall and thin and very strict.

When my grandparents died my mother went to both their funerals. Dad took over whilst she was away; John and I were always hoping that she would not come back for a long time because dad gave us nice things to eat and ice-cream every day after school, which we would not normally have with mum.

We did not have our own house when I was young. We lived in a flat which was in a house over a sweet shop. The place was owned by some rich businessman who would hardly even bother looking at our rent, he was so rich. Nevertheless my mum walked from West Hampstead to Finchley Road every week with the rent. I wouldn't say we were poor. It was just that my parents were saving up to buy our own home that we could call 'ours'. I was very sad when I had to leave the flat. After all I had spent 8 years of my life there. I had had many happy memories there and now I had to leave all those memories behind me.

I started school when I was five years old. I went to a Catholic School. It was a new school in Kilburn called Mason's. We said prayers every morning and also went to Church once a week on either a Friday or a Monday.

Anna Leitrim

IN THE MELTING POT

Hello there; I'm Charmaine Weekes and I live in Paddington, London. The name of my street is Mortimer Road. It is a very long road with houses on both sides. It's not bad really and nearly everybody knows each other. The street consists of mainly all blacks except for a few whites and most of the blacks come from Jamaica.

I am going to put you in the picture of what goes on in and around our community. The number of my door is fifty-six, and it's quite a decent house – all the houses along here are, really.

There are four of us in our family, my mum, dad, bigger brother and myself. We all get on fairly well, although my brother and myself do have a few fights, which is only natural.

All of us are Jams and we came to live in Paddington a few years ago. My mother works in the High Street hairdressers, my father works as a painter and decorator, my brother goes to college, studying engineering, he is nineteen. I go to Park Manor Secondary School; this is a mixed school and it is really great. I am in the fifth year and sweet sixteen is my age. That is all the particulars about my family.

Last night a new family moved next door to us and I am dying to know what they are like.

It's half past seven. I've just finished getting dressed. Breakfast for me is at eight o'clock. My brother and father have already left the house. My mum always tells me not to play records early in the morning but I can't help it; I just love my records.

'Hey madame, how many times me ha' got to tell you not to play those records in the mornings; afore you study something good, you study records. See how far records will put you, me dear.'

Chelsea Herbert

RARE BENGAL TIGER

My first day at school was terrible. I noticed that I was the only Indian boy. There were a few black children. And it seemed that each tribe was segregated. During the course of the following weeks, I tried to mix with the white boys, but they did not want to know. When I asked my father why this was so, he tried to explain to me what prejudice was. I did not understand him.

I would be called Paki, Greaser and various other insults. Boys of my age would come up to me and say 'Paki go home'. Then one day, for no apparent reason, one of them kicked me. I took little notice, although it hurt. He kicked me again, a crowd began to gather.

'Hit him back, Paki', yelled someone.

Hit him back, I thought, but Bapuji always told me that if a stranger or your enemy strikes you on one cheek, show him the other. He had told me to practice *ahimsu* (non-violence), and how could I hit this boy back? He hit me in the face and I stood there. A teacher came and broke up the fight. When I went home that afternoon, father asked what had happened after seeing the bruise on my face. I told him the story and he went to see the headmistress about it. The boy was punished. But that was not the end, only the beginning. I was often beaten up for no reason at all. Father never told me to fight back, until one day I came back with a black eye and a cut lip. From then on he encouraged me to defend myself. At first I was reluctant, but then I saw the necessity. Gradually the bullying ceased and I made friends.

Mayank Patel

Writing project

Now it is your turn. Between now and the end of term you can think about your life. What can you write about yourself and the way you live? You could look at these ideas:

▶ your old schools
▶ family stories, for example about your grandparents
▶ your likes and dislikes
▶ your hopes and fears
▶ you at different times of the day, like breakfast and night-time
▶ your hobbies and games
▶ your tastes in food and drink, TV, and music
▶ your dreams
▶ important events in your life. Some examples of important events in your life might be: moving house, getting hurt, a holiday, school successes, school problems, being a hero or heroine, going on TV or radio, winning or losing something valuable, people getting married, people and/or pets dying.

Take time and care in doing this work. Choose your words and sentences carefully so that the reader finds something interesting to read in your writing. Share your writing; first with a partner, then with pupils from another class or a class at another school.

You do not have to restrict yourself to one form/style of writing in autobiography.

For example, you could produce:

▶ a 'Wanted' poster of yourself, with a factual description of some of your statistics
▶ a map of where you live
▶ a list of your favourite food/drinks/TV/soap operas/pop stars/places/seasons, all with reasons for liking them
▶ a dialogue to show you and other people who are important to you talking about anything you like.

Do not forget to give your reader some information, in any form, about:

▶ your background – family, home, where you were born
▶ what other people remember about you as a child
▶ what you remember as a younger person
▶ important events and people
▶ you and your personality
▶ your future.

If you want to write some of this in dialect, for instance when you are making a dialogue, you may.

Do not forget to draft your work, check your spelling and present your work clearly.

LOOK CLOSELY AT YOUR LIFE. HOW DO YOU WRITE ABOUT YOU?

7 'Teach these children nothing but facts'

Those were the words of Mr Gradgrind, whom you met on p. 46. Sometimes writers have to be very careful to get their facts right. It is a difficult problem to decide about facts, of course.

Discuss and write

With a partner, make a list of the kinds of writing in which facts will be important. Check the lists on p. 40 to refresh your memory about kinds of writing.

You could also look at the list of writing activities on the right produced by a 13-year-old pupil.

Some kinds of writing obviously need to have facts in them: train timetables, telephone directories, instructions for wiring a plug, labelling for poisons or explosives – did you have any of these? One very important feature of factual writing is that everybody who uses the same language can understand it. So it is no use labelling something poisonous unless poisonous is a word in Standard English.

It is also important to present factual information very clearly.

Discuss and write

To make you aware of the difficulty writers of factual information can have, work out with a partner how to write a set of instructions for tieing shoelaces.

Write the instructions after agreeing the form of words you need then try them on the pair next to you. They must follow your instructions just as they are written, and not use their own ideas.

Make a list of the problems encountered.

Now look at this:
A giant sea scorpion, called Pterygotus, lived 400 m.y.a. It was about as long as a car and had huge pincers to catch its food.

Or

Fossils of insects are very rare because their bodies are so delicate. Pine trees leak a sticky liquid, called resin, which often traps insects. Prehistoric resin turns into a transparent, yellow stone, called amber, in which prehistoric insects have been found.

These passages are from a book of facts about prehistoric times. With your partner, discuss these passages briefly. Focus on:
► how the choice of the words, phrases and sentences give the reader the impression of factual writing

KINDS OF WRITING

GRAFFITI
POSTCARDS
ESSAYS
PAMPHLETS
HOMEWORK
MAGAZINES
BLACK BOARD
JOKES
POEMS
LINES
INFORMATION
LISTS
BILLS
NOTES
SIGNATURES
MUSIC
ORDER FORMS
MINUTES OF A MEETING
NEWSPAPER
INSTRUCTIONS
ADDRESS BOOKS
BOOKS (FACT)
EXPLANATIONS
MAPS
SCRIPTS
POSTERS
ADVERTISEMENTS
TICKETS
TIMETABLES
COMICS
GUARANTEES
PRACTISING HANDWRITING
LETTERS
ANSWERS (SCHOOL)
INVITATIONS
JOB APPLICATIONS

WHEN DO YOU NEED TO GET YOUR FACTS STRAIGHT
CAN YOU MAKE POEMS FROM FACTS? TRY IT.

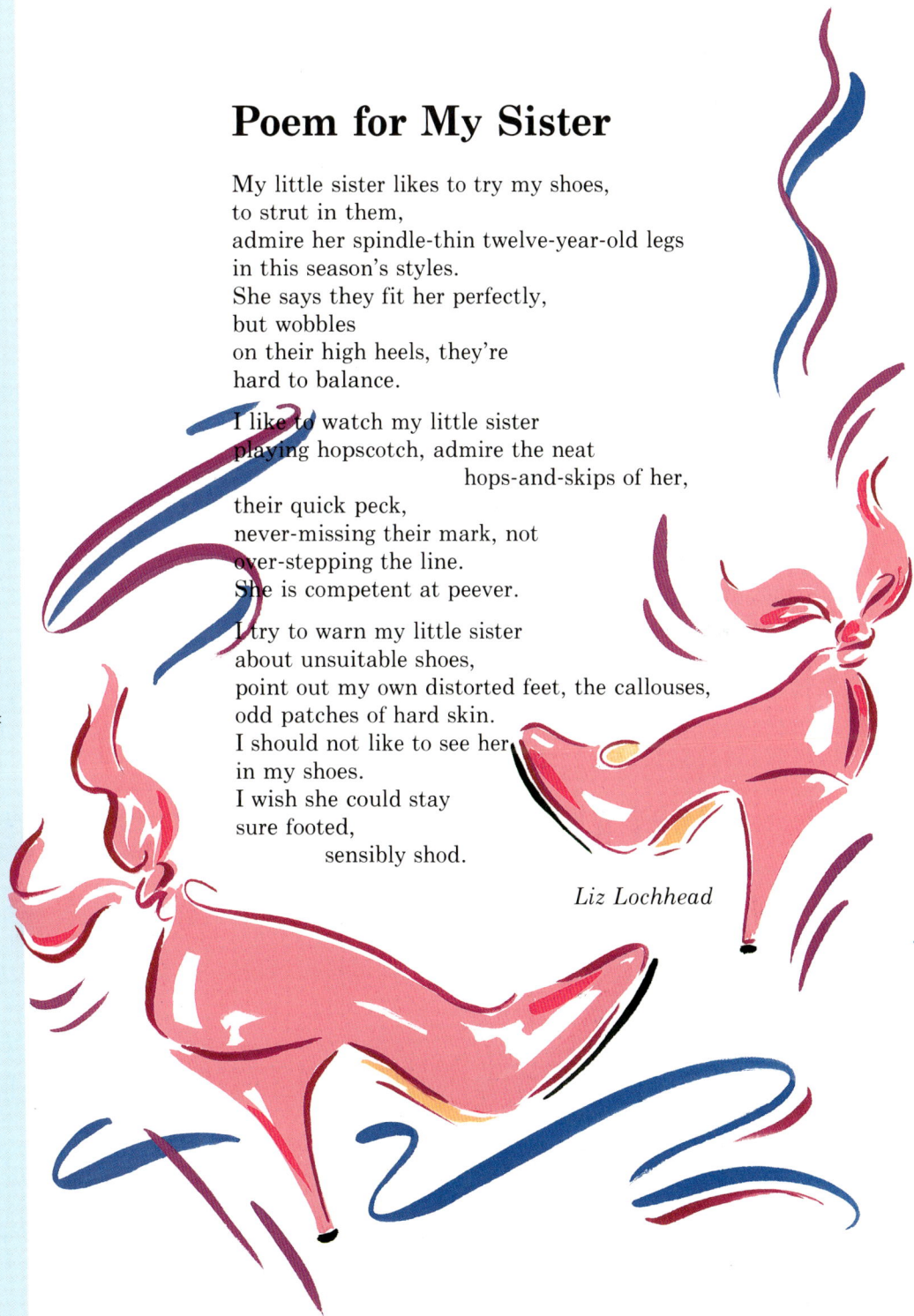

▶ whether you can be sure that the facts are true.

Sometimes we know that certain facts are true, but we behave as if they were false.

Discuss and write

Read the poem by Liz Lochhead. Discuss how the writer uses facts in making her poem. Focus on:
▶ her sister's ability at hopscotch and peever
▶ what fashionable shoes do to feet
▶ how the writer plays with words and moves away from just facts.

In your groups, decide on a topic like smoking, road safety, drugs, pollution or animal welfare. Find out some important facts on the topic and then weave them into a group poem. This will be for an audience of 9–10-year-olds. You are going to make them aware of the topic through writing a poem. When you have made your poems, you could present a reading of them to a class in your local primary school.

Guidelines:
▶ Brainstorm some ideas – one member of the group should act as scribe to write them down.
▶ Try to agree the ordering of ideas to make the poem affect the reader – look back at pp. 33–4.
▶ Discuss your choices of words, phrases and lines, remembering who your audience will be and your purpose in writing the poem.

Poem for My Sister

My little sister likes to try my shoes,
to strut in them,
admire her spindle-thin twelve-year-old legs
in this season's styles.
She says they fit her perfectly,
but wobbles
on their high heels, they're
hard to balance.

I like to watch my little sister
playing hopscotch, admire the neat
                        hops-and-skips of her,
their quick peck,
never-missing their mark, not
over-stepping the line.
She is competent at peever.

I try to warn my little sister
about unsuitable shoes,
point out my own distorted feet, the callouses,
odd patches of hard skin.
I should not like to see her
in my shoes.
I wish she could stay
sure footed,
          sensibly shod.

Liz Lochhead

Look at this extract from a poem called 'Whale Nation' by Heathcote Williams. The writer here is using facts about whales in lines of poetry to get his readers inside the character and life of the whale. He uses words you might not expect in a poem, like 'oscillations', 'laminar'; he uses combinations of words in long phrases to give you the feel of the whale's size.

See if you can use some similar ways of writing in your group poems.

Whales play
For three times as long as they spend searching for food:
Delicate, involved games,
With floating seabirds' feathers, blown high into the air,
And logs of wood
Flipped from the tops of their heads;
Carried in their teeth
For a game of tag, ranging across the entire Pacific.
Play without goals.
Naked,
With skin like oiled silk,
Smooth as glass,
They move at fifty miles an hour.
Attaining faultless streamlining
By subtly changing the shape of their bodies:
Altering ridges of cartilage, and indentations of flesh
To correspond to constantly differing patterns of water;
To accommodate minute oscillations with vibrant inflexions of
    muscle and skin,
So that layers of liquid glide over each other,
In an easy, laminar flow.
No drag, no turbulence.
A velvet energy.

Heathcote Williams

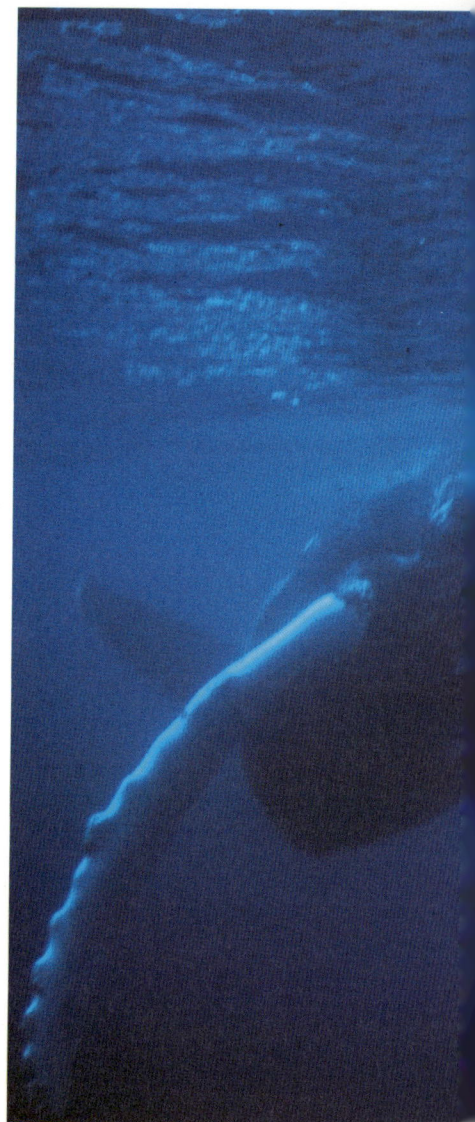

⑧ Putting it all together

☰☰☰ Read and write

Read the story 'The Fall' again (pp. 37–8).
In groups, plan carefully how to make a story like 'The Fall' which uses different kinds of writing in it. See how many kinds of writing you can use without spoiling the story's excitement for the reader. You can make an adventure story, a ghost story, a detective story, a sports story, a science fiction story or any other kind of story.

Try to use kinds of writing you know about first of all, for instance:

▶ postcards
▶ personal letters
▶ instructions
▶ school reports
▶ newspaper headlines or reports
▶ advertisements.

If you try to use kinds of writing you do not know about, ask your teacher to help you find some examples.

You could paste up the finished story on sugar paper and display it on the wall. Make each kind of writing look as realistic as you can. Use real headlines and postcards.

Remember you want to catch the eye of your reader – take

TRY A STORY MADE UP FROM AS MANY FORMS OF WRITING AS YOU CAN. WORK HARD ON HOW TO PRESENT IT.

A really crucial guide to....

Punctuation 2

In Module 3: Writing (p. 52) we looked at capital letters, full stops and commas. What else do you need to know at this stage?

Look at the end of the last sentence. You can see a **question mark**. If you were going to run under a bus, your best friend would probably shout 'Stop!' at you. When you write down urgent, powerful sentences you can end them with an **exclamation mark**. You sometimes see it on warning signs:

Danger! Deadly snakes nearby!

What other ways could you show the same idea, using symbols? Look at some warning signs on your journeys; note down in your writing log the symbols which are used, such as the skull and crossbones. (Design a funny one).

If you see these directions – follow the road five miles E., two S. and three N. – do you know what is going on? E., S. and N. are **abbreviations**, short forms of East, South and North. So keep an eye open for abbreviations. (You might put some in your story in Unit 8.)

Some combinations of words are put together in short forms. These abbreviations do not need full stops after them, as do words like North and South. ANC, ACAS, EEC – find out what these mean and find some more to keep a note of in your logs.

It's^A a dog's^B life!

Notice the circled **apostrophes**. What a long word for a punctuation mark which is tiny, yet annoying to many readers and writers.

Apostrophe A tells the reader that a letter has been left out – It is becomes It's. They're, don't, can't, won't, shan't, – these words all leave letters out.

Apostrophe B tells the reader that the life being written about is that of the dog – it belongs to the dog, not the cat, the elephant or anything else.

Apostrophe B is the belonging apostrophe. With some words, such as plurals, it goes just after the 's', as in cats' dinners, dogs' breakfasts, camels' humps.

With some, you do not use it **at all**: its head, for instance, when describing an undescribable monster.

Try to use some of these punctuation marks in your writing. Try them out on a word processor if you can.

great care with the presentation of your stories. Visitors to your classroom will be reading them. They will expect some good work.

Draft and edit your story using the guidelines in Module 3: Writing, pp. 51–2.

To make your final edit of the story, you need to look carefully at punctuation.

Using the dictionary

When working on the material in this book, there will be times when you want to check spellings and meanings of words. Sometimes you will be able to do this by asking your teacher or your partner; other times, however, you will turn to a dictionary as Roger does below. He has always avoided dictionaries in the past because he finds them confusing and he can never find the words he wants. But really, using a dictionary is quite simple, if you know how.

'Miss, I've been reading this book in History and it says that early roads weren't "macadamized". I don't know what "macadamized" means and I can't find the word in the dictionary.'

'Right. Tell me what you've done to try and find it.'

'I know that the words in a dictionary are arranged in *alphabetical order* and I know that *first and last words* are printed at the top of each page; the first word on the left-hand side and the last word on the right-hand side. So I flipped through the pages until I got to the page that had "lyrical" and "madam" printed at the top, because "macadamize" comes alphabetically between those words."

'Good.'

'But it's not there!'

'Are you sure?'

'There's lots of words printed in a heavy, black print, one of which is the word **macadam** but I can't find "macadamize".'

'Those words printed in **bold print** are called **headwords**. They're printed in a different print to help you pick them out from the rest of the text. You can use the dictionary more quickly that way. Following the headword is the definition – the explanation of the word's meaning or meanings. Lots of words in the English language have more than one meaning.'

'What's that funny word in the brackets immediately after **macadam** miss?'
'This dictionary gives you help with the

pronunciation of difficult and uncommon words. In brackets following some of the headwords you will find them rewritten in the International Phonetic Alphabet. This alphabet is specially designed to show how the different parts of the word are pronounced. If you look at the beginning of the dictionary you'll find out how to use this special alphabet.'

'Miss, there's an *n* after the brackets. Why's that?'

'Most dictionaries use a letter *code* to show you how the word can be used in a sentence. The *n* which is written in italics in this case shows that the word "macadam" is a noun; if you look at the word "macabre", it's followed by an *a*, this shows it's an adjective; the word "macerate" is a verb, and that's represented by a *v* and so on.'

'I know what "macadam" means now, miss, but what about "macadamize"?'

'We'll find it if we first look at the entry for "macadam". "Macadamize" is made from the *base word* "macadam". Sometimes to use a dictionary we have to look up the base word first. Just by looking at the definition of the base word we can make a pretty good guess at the meaning of the word we're looking for. However, if we read the whole entry, we find that some variations made from the base word may also be listed, and in this case the word "macadamize" is.'

'But, miss, although the word's there, it doesn't tell you what it means, it's just got a *v.t.* after it.'

'Yes, that's another example of the letter code. It tells you that "macadamize" is a transitive verb. You can tell if a verb is transitive if you can answer the question "who?" or "what?" after it. So in other words if macadam is a material for road making, macadamize means to make a road from that material.'

'Miss, are all the words in the English language in a dictionary?'

'No. Sometimes the writers of a dictionary leave out old-fashioned words or slang words; sometimes they just select the words you're likely to want to use. That way they keep the dictionary reasonably small. Also words that change when you use them are usually shown just in their base word form. Therefore, on this page, you'll find the word "mad" but you won't find the word "madly" You

have to work out the meaning from the base word. It's easy really. You just have to get to know your way round the page.'

writer's emotions; (of poet) writing lyric poetry. *n.* lyric poem; (often in *pl.*) words of song. **ly′ricism** *n.*

lyrical (lı′rıkəl) *a.* resembling or using language appropriate to lyric poetry; *colloq.* highly enthusiastic.

M

M, m, *n.* Roman numeral 1.000.
M. *abbr. Monsieur*; motorway.
m. *abbr.* maiden (over); male; married; masculine; metre(s); mile(s); million(s); minute(s).
ma (mɑ) *n. colloq.* mother.
M.A. *abbr.* Master of Arts.
ma'am (mæm) *n.* madam (esp. used by servants or in addressing royal lady).
mac: see **mack**.
macabre (məkɑ′br) *a.* gruesome, grim.
macadam (məkæ′dəm) *n.* material for road-making with successive layers of broken stone compacted; tar macadam. **maca′damize** *v.t.*
macaroni (mækərəʊ′nı) *n.* pasta formed into long tubes; 18th-c. dandy.
macaroon (mækəru′n) *n.* biscuit of ground almonds etc.
macaw′ *n.* kind of parrot.
mace[1] *n. Hist.* heavy usu. spiked club; staff of office; staff symbolizing Speaker's authority in House of Commons.
mace[2] *n.* dried outer covering of nutmeg used as spice.
macédoine (mæsıdwɑn) *n.* mixture of fruits or vegetables esp. cut up small.
macerate (mæ′səreıt) *v.* make or become soft by soaking. **macera′tion** *n.*
Mach (mɑk) *n.* ~ **(number)**, ratio of speed of body to speed of sound in surrounding medium.
machete (mətʃe′tı) *n.* broad heavy knife used in Central Amer. and W. Indies.
Machiavellian (mækıəve′lıən) *a.* unscrupulous, cunning.
machination (mækdıneı′ʃən) *n.* (usu. in *pl*) intrigue; scheme, plot.
machine (məʃi′n) *n.* apparatus for applying mechanical power, having several

parts each with definite function; bicycle, motor cycle, etc.; aircraft; computer; controlling system of an organization. *v.t.* make or operate on with machine (esp. of sewing or printing). ~**-gun**, mounted gun, mechanically loaded and fired, giving continuous fire; ~ **tool**, mechanically operated tool for working on metal, wood, or plastics.
machinery (məʃi′nərı) *n.* machines; mechanism; organized system, means arranged.
machinist (məfi′nıst) *n* person who works (esp. sewing-)machine.
machismo (mətʃı′zməʊ) *n.* virility, masculine pride.
macho (mæ′tʃəʊ) *a.* ostentatiously manly or virile.
mac(k) *n. colloq.* mackintosh.
ma′ckerel *n.* edible sea-fish. ~ **sky**, dappled with rows of small white fleecy clouds.
ma′ckintosh *n.* cloth waterproofed with rubber; coat etc. of this or of any waterproof material.
macramé (məkrɑ′mı) *n.* art of knotting cord or string in patterns; work so made.
macrobiotic (mækrəʊbaıo′tik) *a.* relating to or following diet intended to prolong life.
ma′crocosm *n.* universe; any great whole.
mad *a.* with disordered mind, insane; frenzied; wildly foolish; infatuated; *colloq.* annoyed. ~**cap**, reckless person; ~**house**, mental home or hospital, *fig.* confused uproar; ~**man**, ~**woman**, mad person, **ma′dness** *n.*
madam (mæ′dəm) *n.* polite formal address to woman; *colloq.* woman brothel-keeper; conceited etc. young woman.

Glossary

Adjective a word used to describe a noun in more detail:
e.g. the book
    the **red** book

Adverb a word used to say something more about a verb:
e.g. she swam **quickly** towards him

Accent the way we pronounce words. This usually depends on the country we come from and the region we were born in or live in.

Audience the person (or people) who read what we write or who listen to what we say.

Autobiography a written account of your own life.

Base word a word to which other words, suffixes and prefixes are added to make new words:
e.g. the base word **man** can be used to make new words by adding:

a suffix '-ly' – '**man**ly'
a prefix and a suffix 'un' and 'ly' – 'un**man**ly'
another word 'sea' – 'sea**man**'

Characters the people in stories, poems and films, etc.

Contents page the page found at the beginning of a book or magazine. It lists the sections or chapters that make up that book or magazine.

Dialect the form of language which is spoken by a group of people, living in a specific area. There are lots of different dialects in the English language, which use different words, different rules for putting words together and different ways of pronunciation.

Draft the rough, unpolished version of a piece of writing.

to edit to make corrections to a piece of writing.

Form the way in which a story or an idea has been set down by a writer.

Headword the name given to a word listed in a dictionary. The headword is followed by an entry, which records its meaning, its use, its pronunciation and its related words and their meanings.

Images used by writers to help us picture in our minds what is being described. Images are usually based on comparisons and help us to see in a fresh way what the writer is describing:
e.g. 'The teacher had a nose **like a conker**'
or
'He **scythed** his way through the crowded penalty area.'

Index a list in alphabetical order at the end of a book which records the subjects which the writer has referred to.

Key word or phrase a word or phrase that sums up a topic or theme.

Noun used to name a person, a place or a thing – policeman, town, pen.
Abstract nouns name ideas and feelings – justice, love, friendship.
Concrete nouns name things you can recognise through your senses – pepper, sand, scream, heat, view.
Proper nouns are the names we give to specific people and places – Nigel, Holly, Kerry, Cheltenham, Worcester, River Thames.

Prefix a unit of one or more letters added to the beginning of a base word to make a new word:
e.g. sympathetic + prefix **un** makes the new word '**un**sympathetic'
appear + prefix **dis** makes the new word '**dis**appear'

Pronunciation the way in which we speak the words and sentences of a language.

Purpose	the reason why we speak, listen, read or write.
Register	a style of speech or writing which is used by certain groups of people or in certain situations. For example, groups of teenagers use a teenage register which includes words like 'ace', 'brill', 'hunk'.
Rhythm	the sense of beat you hear in a line. Poets often try hard to create a rhythm in their poems.
Rhyme	the repetition of similar sounds at the end of lines. It is usually found in poetry but writers of newspapers and advertisements use rhyme too.
Scanning	a reading technique that helps you find information in a book without having to read it page by page. You run your eyes over a page looking for a key word or phrase that an author might use when dealing with the topic you are interested in. When you find your key word or phrase, you return to the beginning of the section of the book you found it in and read the whole section in close detail.
Skimming	when you read quickly through a piece of writing to get the gist of it.
Standard English	a dialect which is used in public life and in formal situations. The language used in school, in law, in TV, radio and newspapers is Standard English.
Suffix	an ending which when added to a word either shows you what part of speech the word is, changes the meaning or shows you how the words within a sentence or phrase relate to one another: e.g. man + suffix **ly** makes the adverb 'man**ly**' thought + suffix **less** make the new word 'thought**less**'
	Rebecca + suffix **'s** shows you that the pens in the phrase 'Rebecca**'s** pens' belong to Rebecca
Redraft	the reworking of an early version of a piece of writing.
Text	any written material which has an audience and a purpose.
verb	a word that tells you what someone or something does, feels or is. A **transitive verb** has an object – something or someone is affected by the action or feeling described by the verb: e.g. I **kicked** the ball. (**kicked** is a transitive verb, having ball as its object) An **intransitive verb** is a verb without an object: e.g. It rained.

Answers

Module 2, Unit 8, p. 36
The missing words are: Crimbo, bruv, geezer, Yankee Doodle Dandy land, mates.

Module 5, Unit 8, pp. 104–7
The crime was committed by Lesley Harris.

Acknowledgements

The authors and publishers wish to thank the following who have kindly given permission for the use of copyright material:

Allan Ahlberg for extract from *Woof!*, Penguin Books Ltd, p. 9 • Maya Angelou for extract from *I Know Why the Caged Bird Sings*, Virago Press Ltd, pp. 11–12 • Peggy Appiah for 'How wisdom was spread throughout the world' from *The Pineapple Child and other Tales*, Andre Deutsch Ltd, pp. 44–5 • Margaret Atwood for extract from *Cat's Eye*, Bloomsbury Publishing Ltd, pp. 17–18 • Leila Berg for extract from *Look at Kids*, pp. 72–3 • James Berry for 'Becky and the Wheels-and-Brake Boys', Hamish Hamilton Ltd, pp. 94–5 • Betsy Byars for extract from *Eighteenth Emergency*, The Bodley Head, pp. 90–1 • John Cleese and Connie Booth for extract from *Fawlty Towers*, p. 121 • Cyclists' Touring Club for extract from *Positive Cycling*, pp. 100–1 • Kathleen Dayus for extract from *Where There's Life*, Virago Press Ltd, pp. 70–1 • *Early Times*, the independent newspaper for young people, for letter, p. 35 • English and Media Centre for extracts from *Our Lives, Young People's Autobiographies*, pp. 124–7 and *City Lines*, pp. 10, 97 • Anne Fines for extract from *Crummy Mummy and Me*, Andre Deutsch Ltd, p. 122 • Fleetway Publications, for 'The Secret Diary of Hadrian Vile' and 'Natlays', pp. 118, 123 • Roger Green for extract from 'The Devil Finds Work', Oxford University Press, pp. 107–8 • Adrian Henri for 'Best Friends', p. 30, and 'Africa', p. 33, from *The Phantom Lollipop Lady*, Methuen • The *Indy* for letter, p. 35 • International Music Publications for 'A Clean Sweep', pp. 68–9 • Laurie Lee for extract from *Cider with Rosie*, The Hogarth Press, p. 3 • Alison Lurie for 'Gone is Gone' from *Clever Gretchen and other forgotten folk tales*, William Heinemann Ltd, p. 59 • Wes Magee for 'Week of Winter Weather' from *The Witch's Brew and other Poems*, Cambridge University Press, p. 34 • Jan Mark for 'Send Three and Fourpence We Are Going to a Dance' from *Nothing to be Afraid of*, Kestrel Books, pp. 84–8 • Roger McGough for 'First Day at School' from *In the Glassroom*, Jonathan Cape, p. 3 • Thomas Nelson and the School Curriculum Development Committee for extract from the *National Writing Project*, pp. 41–2 • R. Ogley for extracts from *In the Wake of the Hurricane*, Froglets Publications, p. 112 • Oxford University Press for extract from the Little Oxford Dictionary, p. 133 • Penguin Books Ltd for cover illustrations of *Trouble Halfway* and *What Katy Did at School*, p. 93 • Michael Rosen for 'In the Playground' from *When Did You Last Wash Your Feet*, Andre Deutsch Ltd, p. 32 and 'Chivvy' from *You Tell Me*, Kestrel Books, p. 67 • The Society of Authors as the literary representative of the estate of W. W. Jacobs for 'The Monkey's Paw', pp. 24–8 • D. C. Thomson & Co. Ltd for extract from *Jackie*, p. 36 • Usborne Publishing Ltd for extract from *Giants*, pp. 55–6 • Heathcote Williams for extract from *Whale Nation*, Jonathan Cape, p. 130 • Victoria Wood for extract from *Up To You, Porky*, Methuen, p. 120 • Wood Green Animal Shelters for advertisement, p. 23.

We are also grateful to the following for permission to reproduce photographs and artwork:

AA Photo Library, p. 82 • BBC, p. 121 • Birmingham Reference Library, Local Studies Department, p. 71 • Cheltenham Bournside School, Tejal Patel and Sally Birchley, pp. 102–3 • Cliffe Castle Museum, p. 108 • Mary Evans Picture Library, pp. 77, 80, 117 • Sally and Richard Greenhill, pp. 30–1, 66, 73 • Greenpeace, p. 23 • Halfords, pp. 100–1 • Imperial War Museum, pp. 115–16 • Frank Lane Picture Agency, p. 110 • National Gallery, p. 50 • *Oldham Evening Standard/ Graham Collin*, p. 108 • Panos Pictures, p. 33 • P&O European Ferries Ltd, p. 14 • Planet Earth Pictures, pp. 130–1 • Raleigh, p. 100 • Scope Features, p. 36 • Syndication International, p. 112.

Every effort has been made to trace all the copyright holders, and we apologise if any have been overlooked.